emotional
virtue

emotional
virtue

A GUIDE TO DRAMA-FREE RELATIONSHIPS

by sarah swafford

Totus Tuus
PRESS

Published by Totus Tuus Press
PO Box 5065
Scottsdale, AZ 85261

Cover design by Devin Schadt
Back Cover portrait by Laura Wills Photography.
Typesetting by Loyola Dataworks
Printed in the United States of America

ISBN 978-0-9913754-5-5 (hardcover)
ISBN 978-0-9913754-6-2 (paperback)
Library of Congress Control Number: 2014957371

For my Lord, my husband, and my children
I couldn't have done this without you
I love you

CONTENTS

INTRODUCTION

It was a cold night in February, and as I put on my coat to head out the door, I couldn't seem to shake the butterflies in my stomach. For months I had sat around coffee mugs and cafeteria trays listening and talking to college men and women about life. I had taken a job as a Residence Hall Director at Benedictine College and I was responsible for 142 beautiful freshmen college women. Through homesickness, failed exams, spontaneous dance parties, ramen noodles in the drinking fountain, sledding injuries, the excitement of new relationships—and often the heartache of breakups—I had a front row seat for the highs and lows, the joys and sorrows of transitioning from high school to college; a front row seat not only for observing the women, but the men as well, and especially watching them interact together.

In those years, my amazing husband, Andy, our small children, and I all made our home in the cozy little apartment down the hall and to the left of the elevator in that freshmen women's dorm. The men and women knew where to find us—we were there for them; we shared life with them, and we loved it.

As a wife and young mother not too far removed from college, it was easy for me to remember the struggles and victories of my life BM—"before marriage." As I listened, sometimes late into the night, I felt as though I kept giving the same advice, whatever advice I could, over and over

9

again. And then one night, a group of girls said, "Alright, Sarah, you've got to give a talk on all *this* . . ." "What do you mean by all 'this'?" I replied. "You know, 'this'!" We couldn't even put a name to it, but we did seem to talk about "this" all the time!

So, right around St. Valentine's Day—that seemingly wretched day loathed by those who happen to find themselves single—I posted some flyers around campus for a talk. In bold letters, the posters read: "LOVE, EMOTIONS, MENTAL STALKING, AND MR. RIGHT."

As I walked across campus that night, I was trying to get a grip on my nerves! Since I was the kind of person who would shake like a leaf even trying to *read* in public, I knew this was going to be a stretch for me. I was hoping that maybe twenty girls would show up and we could have a great conversation. But when I walked through the doors of the auditorium, there were *almost three hundred women* waiting for me. I couldn't believe it. All I could think was "Wow, we must be onto something!" I was very real with the women that night—I spoke about competition, image, dating, relationships, and how to try to sort through life with as little drama as possible. After all, life is already pretty dramatic on its own.

The question-and-answer session after my talk went on for hours. As I walked back across campus to my apartment, I could see groups of women huddled around each other in deep conversation. To say I stirred the pot would probably be an understatement. When I got back to my apartment, there was a line of girls sitting in the hallway waiting for me. My husband, standing in the doorway, looked at me wide-eyed and asked, "What did you say?" I just laughed and explained, "I don't know! I was so nervous, I don't really remember!"

After that night, I knew the women were hungry. They were hungry for answers, hungry for truth—and most of all, hungry for a change. They were tired of the games, tired of the heartache, and exhausted from the drama. Every woman in that room had a different, yet similar story; and for the first time, many of them were ready to share it with one another.

"I feel like a mess inside," some admitted. "On the outside I have it all together, but when I am alone with my thoughts, it's not a good place to be." Others said, "I'm tired; I'm tired of running away from myself. I'm tired of pretending. I don't even know who I am." Or: "I feel so alone. I know this guy is not the answer; I know that he's not the one, but I keep going back to him."

After the talk that night, the conversation spilled over to the men on campus as well. Many of them came to me and Andy, wanting to know more, sharing their struggles, and just trying to figure out life.

Whether you are in junior high, high school, college, or out of college—really at any age—life can be a wild ride. At the end of the day, we all desire to love and to be loved. But as simple as that may sound, it might be the most complicated, tangled up mess we will ever have to endure.

To make matters worse, the pressure to be "perfect" by the world's standards and the pressure to date breathe down the necks of many men and women. The endless chase to "keep up" and not be left behind, or left alone, drives much of the world we live in—creating a sense of fear, insecurity, and worry that we'll just never be enough, that we'll never be truly loved. I understand this fear, and I've been there. It's scary, but you are not alone.

When I gave that talk on that cold night in February, it was like I threw a grenade; and it started a conversation, one that needed to take place. It can be so easy to feel like you are the only one struggling, the only one who feels alone or unwanted. People often wear an array of different masks and build fortresses around their hearts in order to portray and protect a certain image. The wounds and pain from the past make it seem as though it's not worth the risk of letting anyone in. So many people walk around carrying so much, all the while smiling and pushing "play" on the automated response—"I'm fine, I'm good, everything's great."

There has to be another way—another way to tackle the pain, another way to tackle life, and another way to pursue love, by allowing ourselves to be loved and to love others. That's why I wrote this book, as an attempt to find an alternative plan, with the hope of moving the conversation forward. And this book is for both men and women, because we are all in this together.

This book is the fruit of thousands of conversations with men and women from many different stages in life. I am not an expert, and this is not meant to be an academic book or even a research article. It's this simple: if I could grab lunch with you, have a cup of coffee with you, or write a letter to you, this book is what I would want you to know.

In Part I (The Attack: Where Is All This Coming From?), we'll take a deeper look into what seems to be "messing" with us—the pressures, insecurities, fears, and sources of frustration and confusion. Sometimes laying out the ugly and brutal truth about what we are up against helps us to understand more clearly how it is affecting us. We have to be honest about the current conditions on the ground; otherwise, we'll run the risk of being blindsided.

In Part II (The Answer: Where Do We Go from Here?), we will look at life in light of the attacks of Part I and move forward with a new awareness and a new plan—a plan for life and love, giving us not only a fresh outlook, but also offering practical ways to live it out.

In the final part of the book, Part III (The Avenue: A Roadmap with the End in Mind), we will build upon everything we've laid out and use this new awareness to navigate relationships, figuring out how to move from "Hey" to "I Do." Relationships can be ridiculously complicated these days, and it is no secret that social media and texting are changing dating in the twenty-first century. As one frustrated college guy put it: "Why isn't there some kind of instruction manual for dating? A formula, blueprint, outline, finger-paint drawing—anything! How are we supposed to just know what to do?"

While some of you may be tempted to skip ahead to this last part on dating and relationships, I ask that you start at the beginning; each chapter builds on the previous one, creating a foundation and framework in which to understand and experience the thrill of dating. And I don't want you to miss out on this wider picture by jumping ahead.

By the end of this book, I hope that you will hold in your hands more than just a "finger-paint drawing." I hope you will hold in your heart and mind some answers—not just about relationships, but also about the real questions of life, as you strive to become the person you truly long to be.

PART I: THE ATTACK

WHERE IS ALL THIS COMING FROM?

1

THE WORLD'S IDEA OF PERFECT

As I sat in a high school cafeteria sharing hot roast beef and instant mashed potatoes with a group of young men and women, I couldn't help but notice the glances around the room. I had just given a talk to the student body and they invited me to lunch. It seemed as though there was a sign on each table identifying the various cliques: "Jocks," "Popular Girls," "Intellects," "Artists," "Techies," "Goody Two-Shoes," "Dark and Brooding," "Gamers," and so on. I hadn't been in a school cafeteria in a while, but even I was uneasy.

You could smell the intimidation; competition was high and self-esteem levels appeared to be low. On full display were the darting eyes, stares, laughter, heads down, heads held high, and so many other spoken and unspoken cues. I brought it up with the people at my table, and as we all gazed across the cafeteria, one of the girls said, "You're either in or you're out, and if you're out, you're invisible." She said it so simply and without hesitation; it was a fact of life for her. But yet those words meant so much more than just a matter-of-fact observation.

The first part of this book is called "The Attack" for a reason. I should warn you upfront, this could get ugly. I probably don't need to caution you, because you will unfortunately know exactly what I mean. As I listen to men and women across the country talk about their lives and different struggles, I have to be honest, I worry. I worry, because the world likes to mess with you.

For the men, the world bombards you with an image of what a "real man" is supposed to be and do: control, dominate, uphold the ego, and succeed at anything and everything, or else risk being deemed a complete failure. And for the women, you have models and celebrities handing out a checklist of the "perfect woman" to keep up with. Whether you are a man or a woman, the world throws a lot of requirements at you in order to "make the team." Then we add in a little competition here, some comparison there, throw in some body-image insecurities, sprinkled with the pressure to find, date, and keep "the one"—and you've got a recipe for disaster.

This is the five-ton elephant in the room—everyone sees it, tries to talk around it, and then pretends it doesn't exist. So what exactly is *it*? It is the thoughts, fears, anxieties, and insecurities that no one—and I mean no one—dares to admit or acknowledge, maybe even to themselves. Sometimes this fear is absolutely paralyzing, invading our minds with thoughts like these:

"I'm not enough, I will never be enough. If I only had _____."

"No one will ever love me and accept me, especially now that I've _____."

"If only I could get their attention, if only they could 'see' me, then I'd _____."

"He's got everything he wants, all he has to do is snap his fingers and _____."

"It's so easy for her, she doesn't have to deal with _____."

In our quiet moments, we might wonder, "Where are these thoughts coming from? Why does it feel like I'm always being attacked, or sometimes attacking someone else in my own mind?" It seems to be humanity's quiet, secret struggle. Man or woman, no one is immune; and no one gets out unscathed or unharmed.

Upholding the Image

There is so much pressure to be perfect. It's a battle with what I call the "World's Idea of Perfect." I don't know who has the authority to create it or what machine cranks out this list of perfect attributes, but there it is—holding everyone in check (and at ransom), and everyone knows it.

Life is about being in the perfect place, at the perfect time, with the perfect group of people, so that you can take the perfect picture—edit it, filter it, and then post it for everyone to see. The goal in life is to keep up: to dress, act, present, and even post, the perfect image of yourself. This image is everything; it is exactly what the world (and seemingly everyone else) judges you by. Whether you are 13, 16, 23, 31, or 51—it doesn't matter—you've got to keep up with the World's Idea of Perfect.

For the women, it may look a little something like this: size negative two, big doe-shaped eyes, elongated neck and legs, voluminous lips and hair, killer wardrobe, large circle of followers, attention from all the guys, a popular boyfriend—oh yes, and this perfect boyfriend adores her and spends every waking moment trying to make her happy. And most important of all, not only does she look good doing it—*everybody knows it.*

For the men, I get this image of a guy in a white tux with dark shades standing on a car with women crawling up his legs, stacks of cash lying around, and he's pumping his fist in the air. Okay, just kidding, but that image does come to mind! A man has to be rugged, chiseled, charming, assertive, the leader of his followers, totally in control at all times, and of course accompanied by the gorgeous trophy girlfriend on one arm. All the men want to be him, and all the women want to be with him—*and everybody knows it.*

Okay, there it is, out in the open for everyone to see. And I must say, good luck with *that*. It sounds like a lot of work; and if you've got it, you had better not mess it up. You wouldn't want to gain ten pounds, take a bad picture, get a bad haircut, or have an angry friend spreading rumors and lies about you—or the unthinkable, to be dumped by the perfect boyfriend or girlfriend. Everyone knows that the World's Idea of Perfect can be here one day and gone the next, leaving you confused, broken, and alone. Everything that you had built up and worked so hard to get can come tumbling down around you and be gone in an instant. Indeed, obtaining and maintaining this image is a full-time job.

This is just a glimpse into a few criteria on the checklist for the World's Idea of Perfect, and I am sure that based on where you come from, it may look a bit different; but the demands, image, and pressures are still much the same —the bar has been set, and it's awfully high.

It is very easy to "see" this reality we are talking about, but we tend not to acknowledge it. I know there was a time in my life when I thought I needed to check off every single box, but I thought it was only *my* little secret. I thought it was the game that I had to play in order to "make the team." I honestly didn't believe that anything else would make me happy, or merit the approval of those around me. I needed to be all things to all people. Keeping up that image was always with me. And the worry and anxiety over losing whatever piece of that image I had worked so hard to obtain scared me; and it seemed to make me work harder, ignoring the feelings and thoughts inside that nagged at me: "Sarah, is this really you? Is this really all you care about? Who are you tirelessly trying to please? Are you truly happy? And why does it seem like something is always missing?"

My favorite method at the time was: ignore, ignore, ignore, push away, rationalize, distract myself, and then run away. When those nagging thoughts of uneasiness crept in, I would turn them off. The pressure to achieve the World's Idea of Perfect was just too great, and I believed that the reward would be sweeter than any longing I might have had to stop this never-ending and all-consuming chase of perfection. Though empty and exhausted, I still kept running after it.

The Real You

Many people confide in me that now with social media and texting, there is the "real you" and the "manipulated, made-up, fantasy version" that you try to portray and project through social media and texting. Often, the "real you" is almost unknown—to others, and even perhaps to yourself.

Isn't it amazing what this drive for perfection can do to someone? It can truly take over: your mind is always fixated on it, with every decision based on whether or not something is good for your image, your comfort, your pleasure, your status. And while you are consumed and paranoid with obtaining and maintaining the World's Idea of Perfect, it typically results in endless competition, comparing, drama, gossiping—which can lead to the tearing down of others, as well as damaging your own interior confidence.

When the World's Idea of Perfect screams at us through media, movies, magazines, or music, women might say to themselves, "Okay, models and celebrities are airbrushed and digitally altered. Supermodels even say they wished *they* looked like themselves!" Or a guy might say, "He has fifty million dollars and can pretty much buy the World's Idea of Perfect and spend all day in the gym!" Even though there is a temptation to compare yourself to celebrities and feel completely inadequate, there is a little bit of a buffer between us and them. But this is not the case when it comes to jumping on social media and endlessly scrolling through your friends' lives. The buffer is gone: you know these people, and you see them almost every day. The comparing and competing is no longer just on reality TV; this is your reality—and this time there is no excuse in your mind for not "keeping up."

Even though men and women don't talk about this five-ton elephant very often, it is there: five tons worth of fear, anxiety, emptiness, and insecurity as people try to keep all their different facades and masks locked firmly in place. And these insecurities and the pressure to keep up give rise to the "games" people play: the competition, the comparing, and the tearing down of one another.

Facing Our Insecurities

This competition and comparing can lead to a total lack of trust. Most women don't trust other women because they fear that any vulnerability shown may be used against them, that they might become a chess piece in someone else's game. Men find it hard to be honest and vulnerable with other men; they often fear that showing any sign of weakness will compromise their standing in the eyes of other men. At root, our fears, wounds, and insecurities make it hard for us to trust anyone. Men and women don't want to deal with the potential drama of being emotionally brutalized.

The struggle to achieve the World's Idea of Perfect can consume the heart and mind, leaving one empty and exhausted from trying to attain the unattainable. But when you see someone who seems to "have it all"—the perfect body, the perfect significant other, the perfect group of friends—remember, everyone has a story. No one gets out completely unscathed; and if you look beyond the "perfect image" you will probably see someone just like you, fighting some of the same insecurities and anxieties. They may be hurting also: think of the unbelievable amount of pressure he or she must feel to maintain this image.

So, ladies and gentlemen, the five-ton elephant has been exposed. After bringing all of this to light and listening to countless men and women tell me that they had no idea so many others were also fighting this battle, it's apparent that many people are desperately trying to carry this little secret all by themselves. And I hate to be the bearer of bad news, but this stealthy game doesn't stop at age twenty-five. It can easily be played throughout your entire life.

As you move from one stage in life to another, it doesn't go away—the bullying, cliques, passing nasty notes, and talking behind each other's back in junior high; the "who's talking to who" of high school; the pressure of partying, the "living it up" in college (by the way, the world of perfectionism and status is taken to a whole new level on a college campus)—it all continues throughout life. When you're thrown into the "real world," the competition you once endured with people you went to kindergarten with turns into competition with complete strangers. You battle it out in your career field with successful women in stilettos or men in red power ties; you move into marriage and family, and you find competition among wives, husbands, mothers, and fathers over who has the most beautiful and "perfect" house, wardrobe, spouse, SUV, Christmas card —and unfortunately, children. This continued pressure to be perfect and successful is on full display in social media. And now not only do you have to attain the World's Idea of Perfect, but your spouse (and your children!) need to keep up, too. There is pressure put on them; they grow up with these same "checklists," and the cycle repeats itself from one generation to the next.

I know I just threw a lot at you; I don't know about you, but it makes my head spin and my heart ache. I know that I haven't even scratched the surface, and I certainly don't have this all figured out; but I think we need to start this conversation. I am right here in this fight with you because the fears, anxieties, comparisons, pressures, and the ongoing game of checking off the demands of the World's Idea of Perfect is something we all endure; it seems that just about everyone struggles with aspects of it in one way or another. It's always with us, but now we've brought the five-ton elephant out of hiding. And now that the World's Idea of Perfect has been exposed, it's time to look more deeply into the games we play, in our own hearts and minds, and in our relationships. And so we turn next to what I call the "Emoticoaster."

2

THE EMOTICOASTER

We've all been there before; you stumble upon a boyfriend and girlfriend having a fight in public. You were twenty feet away and you couldn't hear everything, but you just stood in that mall parking lot and watched their body language. Usually the woman is yelling and flailing her arms, pointing her finger into his chest, while the man stands there with his arms crossed or stretched out to the side, with a set jaw and an incredible look of confusion on his face. It seems as though men and women can have a very hard time understanding one another.

Men will ask, "Why did she react like that? Do *you* know what I did wrong? Why are girls so mean? They are mean to us guys, mean to each other. I just don't get it!" Many men feel defeated when trying to understand women, especially women's emotional lives. Some men just shake their heads, throw up their hands, or walk away.

When I speak to women, the first question they usually ask is, "Why don't guys care? They have no clue how we work, what we need, how to act, what to do. They don't seem to care about life, about us, about anything. They pretty much only care about themselves." Some women will even write men off and project frustration from past encounters upon all men.

Now that we have exposed the World's Idea of Perfect—the struggle with fears, insecurities, anxieties, and pressure—we will turn to the task of digging deeper into how this all plays out in our relationships, especially in terms of how men and women interact with one another.

On the one hand, it is safe to say that men and women struggle with many of the same things in life; after all, we share a common human nature. Still, we would be crazy to think that our differences didn't also play a role in how well we understand—or don't understand—the opposite sex.

I love speaking to big groups of men and women about this topic. I will say to the audience, "Okay, ladies, this is for you . . ." and the men will lean forward and listen intently, thinking "Mmm . . . here it comes, the secret to women—I'll take any help I can get!" The same thing happens when I address the guys. "Gentlemen, this is for you . . ." and the women strain to hear what I'm going to say, pulling out glitter pens and frantically taking notes.

In the spirit of trying to understand one another, let's begin with a look inside "A Typical Friday Night" for the women. Ladies, this is for you. Gentlemen, feel free to grab a pen.

A Typical Friday Night

Ladies, it's Friday night, you just called up a few friends, threw on your sweats, and settled in for a long night of pick-your-favorite-chick-flick movie marathon. Do you go with *Rugged and Handsome, Nerdy and Flirty,* or my personal favorite, *Bad Boy Goes Altar Boy?* Your friends show up with their blankets with sleeves and tackle boxes of nail polish, and it's game on. Two hours of escaping from reality are just what the doctor ordered. But as the closing credits roll, you let out a big sigh and exclaim, "Well, my life is worthless!" Trying to mask your frustration and emptiness, you grab your second box of chocolates and throw on the sequel. After *He's the One: Part II, The Musical,* the desire for entertainment is over; the warm fuzzies have worn off and the daggers are out. You throw the remote control across the room and the emotion turns to rage: "When is it going to be my turn! I am so sick and tired of waiting for Mr. Right to come into my life! I'm tired of being patient! I want a cute guy, on a horse, and a sunset . . . *now!*"

After coming to grips with the fact that you just said all of this out loud in front of your wide-eyed friends, you spend the next couple hours venting together—only to fall asleep exhausted, bitter, and out of double caramel fudge.

The puffy-eyed blank stare that is reflected back to you in the mirror the next morning is an all-too-familiar sight. Trying to push down the feelings and effects from the night before, you methodically get ready for the day, doing everything in your power to distract yourself; but even your "come on girl, get it together" playlist isn't helping this time. You put on your "I'm fine" face, just going through the motions of life, but are constantly bombarded with pictures of happy couples as you scroll up and down on your phone. And then it's Monday morning, and you see him . . . that guy from your history class you are remotely attracted to; he passes you in front of the library and says, "Hi," with a smile. Oh my gosh! Cue the sappy music and round up the bridesmaids! This is it!

So, ladies, what do you do? Well, mentally stalk him, of course. Your heart and mind begins to be consumed by him. You think about your first date—when and how he will ask you out and what the marriage proposal will be like; then you imagine what he smells like, and perform what I lovingly call the "Christmas Card Test." You write your first name with his last name and see how it sounds, and then add all the baby names you adore and make sure that they still have a good ring when combined with his last name. You can't be too careful, you know! Then you move from mental stalking to social media stalking. You devote a solid three hours to looking through his 1,245 pictures. You're mesmerized by his fishing trip with his Dad and Uncle Bill, cooing over his golden retriever. Then you feel your stomach drop when you come across a picture of him with his arm around some girl, and you say to yourself, "Oh, that better be his sister!"

You start flirting with him, and the mental and social media stalking goes on for a while, and then you get the guts to do some detective work. Your mission: Get the cell phone number—it's time to text. After texting for a while, you hit the little green button and actually call him. This is followed by a string of nights where you stay up till two o'clock in the morning on the phone. Then eventually you start physically stalking him: you have to be with him, by his side, at all times. And all of this came from just a little "Hi" in front of the library.

One Wild Ride

All the ladies out there probably just awkwardly giggled and turned a little red at the truth of this "Typical Friday Night" and its aftermath. And all the men are probably in a bit of a daze going, "Wow . . . that's not what my typical Friday night looks like, but that does explain a lot. And just what is this 'mental stalking' again?"

This Typical Friday Night illustrates what I call the Emoticoaster. It can be like a rollercoaster. You pay fifty bucks to get into the amusement park, walk about ten miles, taking in the smell of funnel cakes and the hot asphalt burning through your flip-flops; then you wait in line for three hours for the ride of your life. You get a little closer to the front, hand over your ticket, and say to yourself, "This is going to be epic!" You're strapped in, ready for the steep climb chink, chink, chink, chink; up and over the top, the ride throws you headlong down the hill; you are knocked from side to side, whiplashed, with tears streaming down your face from the wind. And then the ride comes to a grinding halt, and your head is thrown back against the seat. You take one step off the ride and throw up in front of everyone. For the next hour or so you sit on a bench under a shady tree by a trash can and ask yourself, "Why did I think that was going to be a good idea?"

The Emoticoaster can send you on quite a ride. It may look a little different and move at different speeds but the Emoticoaster is a reality for both men and women. It is how a lot of relationships begin, and unfortunately often end. You may be thinking, "C'mon Sarah, mental stalking, social media stalking, flirting, texting, calling, and physically stalking are all just part of the gig." In some ways perhaps, but before you buy the "All Day Pass" and the "Season Ticket Bundle," let's take a look at some of the potential traps and pitfalls.

First, *mental stalking* is a one-way relationship. You are building the unknown, expectations can be high, and let's be honest, it can be a little creepy.

With *social media stalking*, you are getting into someone's personal life and making assumptions. Wouldn't you rather let the person tell you about himself or herself?

Flirting (whether in person, text, or through social media) can be tricky. It's hard not to come across as fake. Don't you want the person to get to know the *real* you? Seeking and getting attention is one thing, but it's easy to send mixed messages that can sometimes turn ugly in the end —since it's not difficult for friendly flirting to come across as a sensual comment, one that you may not have initially intended. Or, sometimes it is just that: flirting in a joking way is often a less risky type of sensual advance, trying to test the waters, so to speak, to see if the interest is mutual. This type of flirting (where friendliness, joking, and sensual advances are combined) can lead others to question, "Who is this person, really?" simply based on the way someone interacts with the opposite sex.

Texting, oh texting. Texting can be intimate and easily misinterpreted; people often rationalize messages sent (or received) via text that they would never say in person. It's hard for a text to convey verbal and nonverbal cues that happen effortlessly in face-to-face communication. Texting can also be very addictive. Many people confide in me that it "just does something to them inside" when their phone lights up every two minutes.

Calling—although it's good to talk on the phone with the intention of getting to know someone, calling up a crush and lying in bed with the phone to your ear until two in the morning can put you in a very vulnerable spot and can be very revealing. Texting and talking late into the night can create a sense of emotional intimacy and closeness that may not be as deep as it may feel.

Finally, *physically stalking*. You probably think I mean following someone around like a puppy dog; but by physically stalking, I mean when you feel as though you have to be around this person and can't have any fun without him or her. You start doing things just because he or she is doing them and going places just because he or she is there.

We have all seen people drop their friends and virtually change who they are in order to please the new love interest in their life. Emotions and passions can be so strong, making it easy to get swept away before you even realize what has happened.

As we can see, the Emoticoaster can definitely be a wild ride, and one that we would do well to be on the lookout for before we buy the "Season Ticket Bundle," as we said earlier. While daydreaming, texting, social media, talking, and flirting may be part of any present-day romance story, you have to go into this with eyes wide open. There are certainly times when you can follow your heart, but don't forget to bring your head with you!

Whether it's the three-hour wait in anticipation of the thrill or the ride itself, something "sends" people onto this ride over and over again—and it often does so without our even realizing it. Though it may be a bit different for everyone, something is feeding this desire to take this ride —something I call the "Cycle of Use."

3

THE CYCLE OF USE

Have you ever read the lyrics to a love song or a rap song —no music, just printed out the lyrics and read them out loud? They usually go something like this: "I want you." "You don't know you're beautiful." "Baby, just say, 'Yes.'" "Give it to me." "This feels right." "I can take away your pain."

The media likes to play on your emotions and passions. Movies, music, magazines, television, video games, apps, books, social media—all these things can influence your desires, wants, and needs. And media certainly caters to men and women differently, because they know what sells.

Women are usually enamored with what they hear and can easily use their imaginations to put themselves in the place of a character. Whether it is the damsel in distress at the box office, the woman being serenaded in the love song, or the main character in a romance novel—these scenes all evoke a rush of emotion and passion that takes you somewhere enchanting and allows you to escape from yourself for a moment.

Men are typically more visual and turned on by what they see. Epic war battles, fast souped-up cars, and saving the planet from aliens—these usually make the list of what makes excellent "guy media." Typically something blows up about every five or six minutes and there is at least partial nudity, if not a sex scene (or several). The media is ready and willing to give men "action"—visual entertainment and pleasure in a variety of forms—and of course, it all sells.

Now a word on stereotypes: I am not saying that women aren't turned on visually. There are many women who struggle with the onslaught of shirtless men popping up on their phones or on the big screen. And men are not always the stereotypical, heartless sexual robots who feel no emotion whatsoever. I hear from many men about their emotional struggles, which are in many ways very similar to the stories I hear from women.

Still, women generally tend to be more emotional, sentimental, and attracted to the pleasure of romance; and men generally tend to be more physical, visual, and attracted to sexual pleasure. There are plenty of exceptions, but these stereotypes very often play out in the interaction between men and women.

For this reason, it has been said that "women will often use sex to get love," and "men will use love to get sex." It makes sense. A woman will use her body—what he wants (sex)—to get love; and a man will use the feelings of romance—what she wants (love)—to get sex. And herein lies the Cycle of Use: two people mutually *using* one another, sometimes emotionally, sometimes physically, very often both at the same time. What might *feel* like love often becomes merely the occasion for one person to use the other for a gratifying emotional or physical experience. And sometimes it is the "experience" one is in love with, not the person. This is what is meant by the phrase, "in love with love."

This unspoken (sometimes unrecognized) reality of *use* plays on all those pent-up emotions and passions that have been building up in the heart and mind over time. The woman who has been filling her heart excessively with emotionally saturated movies, music, novels, and daydreaming often seeks to find someone to fill her up emotionally. And the guy who has been filling his head with pornography, movies, games, and music will often look for an outlet sexually. And the man may turn to emotional outlets and the woman to sexual ones as well, in order to fill a void in their heart.

Breaking the Cycle

This is the Cycle of Use. The goal of the man or woman is to attain a certain feeling, or physical pleasure, or some combination of both; and often once that feeling has worn off, the relationship loses its luster. And then the cycle starts all over again—sometimes on and off with the same person, sometimes with someone new.

You've probably seen it before—the couple who continues to break up and get back together, or the guy or girl that has a different partner each weekend. You may have been there yourself in the past, or you may be in the thick of it right now. People on the outside often ask, "Why can't she see that she is being used?" Or, "Why can't he just walk away from her?" Or maybe, "Why can't *I* just walk away?"

It's in our nature, our deepest desire, to love and to be loved. We desire love and happiness more than anything else. And everything we do, we ultimately do in order to fulfill this desire. We don't even like the phrase "to use" because it stirs up something deep inside us that is profoundly uncomfortable with the thought of "using" someone we claim to love. No one looks at another person and says, "I want to use you." Or, "I'm using you." But this is precisely why the mutual using of one another can be so destructive: such use tends to mask itself as love, often making it difficult to recognize.

A girl doesn't text or call up a guy and say, "Hey, I'm sorry to bother you, but I'm feeling alone, and I'd like to use you tonight." Guys don't resort to pick-up lines that include, "You're stunning. Can I use you for about twenty minutes later tonight?" Unfortunately, those texts often go out in some form or another, but the word "use" is usually nowhere to be found. No, the Cycle of Use is much more complicated, much more deceptive, and for that reason all the more damaging.

This may be difficult, but I want you to:

Think about a time when you were used (either physically or emotionally), *and you knew it* . . .

Think about a time when you used someone else (physically or emotionally), *and you knew it* . . .

What about a time when you watched your best friend being used, *and you knew it* . . .

Or, a time when you watched your best friend use someone else, *and you knew it* . . .

Those questions are heavy. We all carry wounds from the effects of being used, and we are wounded from when we have used others as well. Those wounds come from many different places, and they have a tendency to stack upon each other. It is easy to use and to be used without even noticing it, but we have to call it out. It has to stop. We have to break this cycle, the Cycle of Use.

I want you to make the word "use" a new word in your vocabulary, and here's why: we need to recognize use when it happens. We all desire love; and though we might not realize it, settling for use is one of the greatest detriments to true love. You probably already know what "use" feels like; but now you know how important it is to name it, call it out, and devise a plan to break the cycle.

What Sends You?

Part of this battle is knowing what sends you into the cycle, your own personal triggers It's helpful to take a deep look within and honestly list those triggers. Don't be scared of them. Your list may look a little something like this:

> The name of a person, an ex, a friend who pressures you; perhaps it's movies, music, magazines, pornography, "girl talk" or "locker-room talk"; maybe it's drinking, drugs, pictures of shirtless men or pictures of swimsuit models; perhaps feeling pride in being hit on, getting a reaction when hitting on someone else, looking in the mirror, stepping on the scale; or maybe cuddling, sleeping over, sexting; maybe a friend with sexual benefits or a friend with emotional benefits; romance novels, the Internet, channel surfing, mental stalking, social media stalking, texting, and a million other things.

It is important to make your own list. I know it is going to be very difficult, but it's best to be completely honest with yourself. Being aware of your own personal triggers is the first step to breaking the Cycle of Use. I would recommend reading over your list a few times and then try to say this out loud:

> "I will not let anyone *use* me."
> "I will not be *used*."
> "I will not *use* anyone."

Is there anything more beautiful than someone saying, "I will not use you?" For someone to be able to say: "I desire your good, what is best *for you*, not just what seems good for me; I want to think of you and not just myself, I will not use you"—that is one of the most romantic things anyone could ever hear.

Both men and women know the pain of the Cycle of Use, and that is why identifying and coming to grips with the Emoticoaster and the World's Idea of Perfect is so important. These are key because the brokenness and insecurities that result from them are often what propel us into the Cycle of Use.

Hopefully, now that you have seen the World's Idea of Perfect, the Emoticoaster, and the Cycle of Use, you have a new power and a new awareness. In the next chapter, we will use that knowledge and awareness to look at a *Choice* —the Choice to love.

4

THE CHOICE

A few years ago, I gave a talk at a conference for college students who were in fraternities and sororities, and let's just say it was very eye opening. Afterward, I was sitting in the hotel lobby chatting about life with some fabulous college women when a group of guys came back after having gone out on the town. The girls I was with caught their eye and they decided to join us. I had no idea that three hours later I would still be sitting in that hotel lobby learning from a handful of frat boys about what it meant to "get game." Being the naïve country girl from Kansas that I am, I tried not to show my shock and disbelief as they told me story after story about what it was like to be a leader in a fraternity on their campus.

One guy looked me straight in the face and said, "The goal of the weekend is to forget about your worries and just feel good." Another guy chimed in, "You have four years, that's not much time to live it up and make memories." I finally asked, "You keep talking about 'getting game.' What exactly does that mean?'" As I looked around the room, each guy suddenly got a sheepish grin on his face, looking around at the others to see who was going to speak first, or if anyone was going to speak at all. One finally said, "Well, you know, getting game is where you go around and talk to different women to see who is the most . . ."

and then he trailed off. "You know, the most open." "Open to what?" I asked. "Open to sleep with you, open to hook up," he said, in a matter-of-fact sort of way. After a few moments of awkward silence, another guy stepped in:

Basically, you go around the room and learn about different women, what they like, what they are going through, you give them attention, act like you really care and really want to listen and be there for them. Then you tell a few little lies about how you are going through something similar. Then you decide who is the most vulnerable and you zero in on her; since she is the most vulnerable and has already exposed herself to you, there is already an emotional connection there. Once you have established that, you have convinced her that you are a good guy who will make her feel safe and secure. Mix in a little alcohol, her inhibitions are down, and you can close the deal. She wants it, too, it's an easy move.

Wow. As I sat there half-stunned, half nodding my head in sad understanding, my stomach dropped as I looked at the faces of the women around the room. It was as if they all felt violated in some way—exposed and out in the open. No one talked, but I could see each of them reliving some experience of their past. And there it was . . . *use*.

You don't have to be at a frat party to understand what "getting game" is. As we've seen, "use" isn't just physical. A lot of people use each other fully clothed and not even in the same room; I hear story after story of men and women who have three, seven, even ten different people that they are currently "talking" to via text—all of whom become objects of emotional gratification.

A guy may have seven different girls, each thinking she is the only one being pursued. The guy may text for months and then one day just drop her. She thinks to herself, "Why? What happened? What did I do wrong? What's wrong with me?"

Or, it's a girl who has seven different guys she texts in order to be emotionally filled up, to mask her insecurities, her feelings of worthlessness or of being alone. The women tell me that the sensation and surge of worth and fulfillment they get from seeing their phone light up with an incoming text is intoxicating. The words of endearment or desire are like a drug—addictive, always leaving you wanting more. The men I've talked to agree and find themselves drawn to this "intoxication" as well.

The Interior Battle

Women need to understand that men are fighting a very difficult battle. It is essential for every woman to grasp what men are up against. The world tells them to dominate, control, and conquer; take what she will give you; better yet, manipulate her emotionally to get what you want.

In the previous chapter we noted that use is one of the greatest detriments to true love. You can't use a person as a means to an end, and that end cannot be your own emotional or sexual gratification. A woman must not be used as an object for a man's sexual pleasure. He must not use her body, and he does unbelievable damage (both to himself and to her) when he manipulates her emotionally in order to get to her body.

Men need to understand that women are also fighting a very difficult battle. It is essential for every man to grasp what women are up against. The world tells them to do anything to feel loved, secure, noticed, and desired, to do whatever is needed to get and keep this feeling of love.

But a woman must not use a man to fill insecurities, or to make her feel emotionally whole. She must not use him, and she does unbelievable damage (both to herself and to him) when she throws herself at a man physically in order to be filled up by him emotionally.

This is the unspoken use I am talking about, and it can be true for both men and women. And sometimes men and women know it in the depths of their souls; they know they are using someone or are being used, but they decide not to care or think about it. They would rather be used and feel some semblance of love. A guy may know he is physically using a girl, but his own sexual satisfaction trumps her dignity (and his) in that moment. A girl may completely throw herself at a man, because feeling loved, wanted, and not alone trumps his dignity (and hers) in that moment.

This is where the *Choice* comes in. The man and woman both have a choice. Everything that you have read up to this point has hopefully given you a new awareness of the battle that men and women are fighting, their similarities as well as their differences. With this new awareness, we have a choice—*a choice either to help or hurt the opposite sex*. But in order to understand this decision, let's take a deeper look at what *love* really is.

What Is Love?

It seems like a simple enough question. I was reading an article one day and ran across this quote, which captures the essence of what we need to hear:

Love is not *primarily* a feeling, though it can be accompanied by feeling. That's the confusion of our time, confusing love's feeling with love itself. Love actually is a great act of the will. It's when I say, "I desire your good, not for my sake but for yours."[1]

There is something very romantic about this quote; but when you take a closer look, you realize that it is the complete opposite of what the world tells us love is all about. The conversation in your head may have gone something like this:

"Love is not primarily a feeling." Hold up, what? You *fall* in love, right? The emotions and passions overcome you, you can't speak or think straight, and you are in love! But if love is not primarily a feeling, but only "accompanied by feeling," then what is love?

"Love actually is a great act of the *will.*" Wait, I'm confused. I have to "will" it to be in love? I have to work at it? No, no, I fall into the fluffy clouds of love! I am comfortable, and we are good. If I have to work at this, then no thanks, I'm out. This is about me experiencing the feelings of love, and when that is gone, I am gone.

"I desire your good, not for my sake but for yours." I thought everything was for my sake. Isn't this feeling of falling in love about me, about how I feel, about my self-fulfillment? Now I have to desire *your* good —but only as long as it is emotionally or physically satisfying to me, right? I thought love was about this

---

[1] Father Robert Barron, *Catholic Update.* "Being Catholic Today: Light to the Nations," August, 2008.

significant other being all that I desire? I want them to fill me up, take away my fears and insecurities.

I understand that this kind of love is radical. It goes against what we probably assumed love to be, and what we may want love to be—just drinking in and soaking up the feelings of love. But then, there it is—*use*—the three-letter word that keeps creeping in. If we see love only as a *feeling*, then when we long for love, we will be longing for a certain *feeling*; often, unintentionally, we will find ourselves *using* the other person in order to attain these *feelings* of love, a certain emotional or physical experience. And the other person may see love the same way and may be seeking to fulfill a similar desire.

The sad and tragic result is that often what looks and genuinely feels like love is at its foundation a mutual using of one another emotionally and physically. The Choice to radically love is the only way to break the Cycle of Use.

The Test

In the context of mere emotional love or love as only a feeling, it's important to remember that sexual encounters don't clarify things, but only serve to intensify the *feelings* of love—which makes it all the more difficult to see reality in a clear way. The seemingly serious and committed relationship, or the one-night stand, might feel like love; but the all too common heartache afterward shows us that the commitment to one another was not as deep as it might have felt at the time. Here's the test: are my actions helping to foster what is best for the other person, or is it really about me and more about how the other person makes me feel? Is it the *feeling* of love or *true love*? True love is a *selfless* love, not a selfish love. The following quote captures the essence of what we mean here: "The greater the [sense of] *responsibility* for the [other] person, the more true love there is."[2] Feeling responsible for the other person means putting their good first and foremost; what is truly best for the other becomes more important than what I might desire in the moment.

A selfish love is driven more by a desire to feel a certain way, to feel romanced in a certain way—often making the other into more of a fantasy of a person or an experience rather than truly loving and protecting him or her. When a man or woman begins to see that they are truly *responsible* for the soul of another—entrusted into their care, a heart placed into their hands—it completely changes the way they view love.

And so here is the Choice—to love selflessly or selfishly.

In the first part of this book, I have laid out the attacks that most men and women endure—the comparing and competing in the arena of the World's Idea of Perfect, often leading to the Emoticoaster and the enduring pain of the Cycle of Use. And now we have sorted through the confusion about what true and authentic love is, in contrast to love understood merely as a feeling.

This, again, is the Choice: the choice of love over use; the choice not to seek outlets in other people in order to fill the emptiness or void in our own heart, but to love and will their good.

So many men and women tell me, "I know what I *don't* want, and I know what *not* to do. I feel like I am starting to figure out why I am such a mess inside, and the traps I continue to fall into, but now I don't know what *to do*."

---

[2] Karol Wojtyla, *Love and Responsibility*, trans., H. T. Willetts (San Francisco: Ignatius, 1993), 131.

Others say "I am done with the drama, and I'm tired of walking away with baggage from my relationships. I don't want to play games anymore. Please tell me there's a better way."

There is a better way. There are answers, and there is an alternative plan for life and relationships very different from what the world generally has to offer. The first step toward moving in this direction has been to recognize clearly the reality on the ground; our eyes are now opened and we have a new awareness, which has led us to a choice, a choice to love in a selfless way.

Next, in Part II, we are going to lay out a new way of thinking, a new attitude, and a new way of approaching life—a plan to train, prepare, strive, and thrive. You know what you don't want; now it's time to go after what you do want.

PART II: THE ANSWER

WHERE DO WE GO FROM HERE?

5

THE ALTAR SWITCH

You've probably encountered the following conversation at some point in your life: Someone asks you, "How are things going? What are you up to these days? Are you dating anyone?" Often, the emphasis falls to this last question. Whether you are in junior high, high school, college, or out of college, being in a relationship is seen as one of the ultimate status symbols in our society—no doubt rooted in the World's Idea of Perfect.

The pressure could come from friends, the media, your parents, your next-door neighbor, the person who cuts your hair—heck, even your own sweet grandmother! Having a boyfriend or girlfriend is seen as critical to one's social status. To the question "Do you have a girlfriend?" or "Do you have a boyfriend?" the answer is either, "yes," or "no." The person asking doesn't really want to hear any of the details regarding your answer; it's just your "yes" or "no" that seems to matter. If you say "yes," the person asking gives you a playful smirk or smile, her shoulders rise, her chin lifts, and she slaps you on the back, showing you her proud approval. If you say "no," you also get quite a reaction. The person asking presents instant wrinkles in his forehead; he frowns, his shoulders slump, and he hits you on the shoulder and says, "What? Why? Why don't you have one?" And then you have to endure the awkward conversation that follows.

I was chatting with some sophomore high school women when this topic of being single and feeling the pressure to date came up. Most of the girls were currently single and kind of struggling with it. One girl spoke up. "It's all about who you are dating or who is interested in you. It seems to be all that matters." One girl looked at me with a hint of sadness and defeat and said, "Just a few weeks ago, my family and I were sitting around the dinner table and my seventh-grade sister was going on and on about her new boyfriend. My Dad looked at me and said, 'Even your seventh-grade sister has a boyfriend, what's wrong with you? Why don't you have a boyfriend?'"

That Dad may never know or fully understand the profound impact those words had on his daughter. He may not have meant for them to pierce her heart with feelings of worthlessness, but those words deeply affected her and will remain with her for a very long time.

The 80-20 Problem and Its Big Three

Part I of this book dealt with the attacks men and women so often endure—whether in the secret, silent battle with the World's Idea of Perfect, a ride on the Emoticoaster which can be so alluring, or the Cycle of Use which has caused so much damage to the hearts and minds of men and women everywhere. We've called out the culprits and we have a new awareness of what "messes" with us. This pressure to be in a dating relationship only adds to the stress, frustration, and confusion.

Our society seems to worship at the altar of dating and relationships. It's what I call "The 80-20 Problem and Its

Big Three," which goes something like this: single men and women typically worry (or agonize and obsess) about three main questions 80 percent of the time:

1) Who am I going to date and eventually marry?

2) What is he or she going to do for me and how is he or she going to make me feel?

3) How good can I look doing it?

Eighty percent of their time is spent catering to these three questions. The choices they make, big and small, are decided by how well they serve the desired outcome of these questions. You may fall into the 68 percent range or maybe the 95 percent range of worry and mental energy spent, but either way, being consumed with these three questions leaves very little room for anything else.

Despite the intense drive for relationships, there seems to be little concern for the preparation it might take for these relationships to actually go well. I often hear the following from men and women: "Sarah, seriously, it's high school (or it's college). It's time to live it up! I want to make memories! This time in my life only comes along once. I'll settle down later. I'll quit the heavy drinking, the porn, the hookups, the cheating and the partying. I'm not hurting anyone. I will be an awesome person someday, that amazing spouse and parent you talk about. But right now, just let me be."

Regardless of exactly where you fall on the 80-20 spectrum, one thing is most likely the case: we need to pay more attention to that small 20 percent or 10 percent left over and start asking some very important questions.

Whether single or in a dating relationship, many people are hoping and praying for the *Altar Switch*—you know, that magical switch behind the altar. It's like a light switch.

The beautiful bride in her gown stands up in front of the altar and reaches out for the hand of her handsome groom in his bow tie and tux; then before all their family and closest friends they pledge their love to one another, declare their vows, and flip the Altar Switch—*instantly becoming the man and woman, the husband and wife, they always dreamed they'd be.*

But as much as you might want there to be an Altar Switch that would magically turn you into that husband or wife, that father or mother you have always hoped you'd be, that's just not how it works. There is no Altar Switch.

I want that harsh reality to set in, because it is so easy to pretend that the Altar Switch really does exist. There was a time when I wanted it to exist. I thought it would make life so much easier. But it's just not true. The reality is that what you do now *matters,* because you are forming habits that will grow and strengthen over time, either for better or for worse.

Every decision you make, big or small, day in and day out, is taking you closer or further away from the man or woman that you truly long to be. The habits you are forming now are developing your character. Feed bad habits and they grow stronger; feed good habits and they will also grow stronger. As it is commonly said, "Your thoughts become your words, your words become your actions, your actions become your character, and your character becomes your destiny."

The Altar Switch is not real, and who you want to be starts today. Never was this more real to me than the day I was approached by a man after one of my talks. He looked me in the eye and said, "Thank you so much for your talk. You have to keep giving this talk." I said, "Thank you, yes, sure, you know I will." "No, I mean it," he pleaded. "You have to keep giving this talk." He had a very troubled look in his eye as he went on: "You see, I'm a thirty-five-year-old father of the two most beautiful kids. My wife is amazing, but when I make love to her, I don't always see *her*. Sometimes I see a *porn star* because I have been addicted to pornography since I was fifteen years old." He fought to go on. "And if I would have known the pain and struggle this has brought to my marriage, to my wife, I would never have touched the stuff. You have to keep giving this talk."

Before I could say anything, he turned and walked away. My heart ached for him, for his wife, for his family. I knew that I had to carry and share his message, and his message is precisely this: We may not think that the decisions and choices we make right now will affect our future; we may think that the choices we make aren't hurting anyone. But the reality is that what we do now does affect who we are becoming and will therefore affect our life and our future, and even the lives of our future loved ones.

Our present actions have this effect because we are forming our hearts, our minds, our desires, our goals, and our dreams. In other words, *what we let into our minds and hearts now will affect us moving forward.* How we let the pressures and the insecurities and the fears of life play out will affect us, and they will begin to form us.

Real Life's Big Three

The 80-20 Problem is taking up too much space in people's hearts and minds. And so is the attitude of "Let me be, I'll settle down someday." But what would happen if we took the 80-20 Problem and flipped it around? What would happen if people spent 80 percent of their time asking the big questions, the hard questions, the truly life-changing questions, instead of giving only 20 percent of their time to this?

What if we flipped the 80-20 Problem and Its Big Three with what I call "Real Life's Big Three"?:

1) Who do I want to be?

2) What am I living for?

3) Who am I living for?

The world has drowned out these three questions. We are distracted by a million different things that prevent us from asking three of the most important questions in life. What are our goals, dreams, aspirations, hopes, desires —what is our purpose? Whether we are single, dating, engaged, or married, whatever state in life we are in, we have to stop and ask these three essential and life-altering questions, and we need to ask them often.

One of the mottos in the Swafford House is "Don't just survive, thrive!" We all get preoccupied with "just surviving" from time to time, and we don't stop to ask, "Who do I want to be?" "What am I living for?" and "Who am I living for?" To stop and name and claim our *goals* and *roles* is exciting—and maybe even a little scary, because it calls us to greater action on our part.

I know there was a time in my life when I spent about 93 percent of my time agonizing over the 80-20 Problem. I was so worried about being the World's Idea of Perfect, which guy I was going to date, who could give me the attention I craved, how I could fill the insecurities and loneliness I felt—all the while wearing different masks and trying to keep up the facade of "I'm good, I'm fine, everything's great!"

I struggled with the fear of missing out and I was overcommitted and spread too thin trying to be all things to all people. My mind was always running. "What do I need to do next, where do I need to be, and who do I need to be with?" And what's worse, I was so focused on all the ways I wasn't perfect—the ways I wasn't "enough" or didn't have what I wanted—that I didn't take the time to truly ask myself who I wanted to be, what I was living for, or who I was living for.

It was similar for my husband, Andy: captain of the varsity football team, popular, keeping up with friends and the party scene, obtaining and sustaining that "perfect" image —this was his full-time job. A college football scholarship and success on the field made him feel on top of the world, but it all came crashing down when his legs were literally taken out from beneath him early in college. Another football player slid into his leg on a kick return resulting in a broken leg, a shattered image.

The Game of Life

In the months that followed, Andy came face-to-face with the fact that the game he loved and the image he sustained were gone, that his identity was gone. He felt alone, hollow, and depressed. And for the first time in his life, he started asking the tough questions: "Who do I want to be, what am I living for, and who am I living for?"

He knew something had been missing; football was a great game, but it was just that, a game. There was something more, and it took Andy breaking his leg to slow him down and start thinking about a different game, the *Game of Life*.

Andy and I both discovered that we were made for more—more than the drama, the baggage, the anxiety, the "living it up," the world's games. But it wasn't until we started asking the hard questions that we started to find answers, and not just emptiness.

We have to prepare and train for the Game of Life. The place to start is by obtaining self-knowledge—learning who you are, who you want to be, what makes you tick—and then from there forming a plan for where you want to go. No matter where you are in life, it's helpful to take the time to ask these three questions; our answers and our new plan moving forward depend on it. Grab a pen and paper and make three columns and put these headings at the top of each column:

Who do I want to be?	What am I living for?	Who am I living for?

The first time you answer these questions, I want you to do it honestly, based on where you are in life right now. Answer them the way you would have before you ever started reading this book. It might not necessarily be pretty, but it will show you where you stand (or stood). After you have done that, draw a line and rewrite the three column headings:

Who do I want to be?	What am I living for?	Who am I living for?

Now answer these three questions in light of your reading of this book so far. Although some items may have carried over, your new lists may now flow from a different perspective on life. It is essential that these are *your* lists; they can be anything from being more patient with your family, to getting into college, to becoming a leader in your favorite organization, being more present to the people around you, replacing a bad habit with a good habit, having a tough conversation that needs to happen, and so on.

These lists should take into account the different *roles* you play or desire to play in life; listing them out will help you to see the relationships and responsibilities you are committed to: son or daughter, sibling, relative, friend, significant other, student, athlete, musician, employee, leader, coach, or mentor, to name a few. Focusing on these relationships helps us to reorient ourselves to the things that matter most.

Some of you may be in dating relationships or even married; taking the time to do this is just as important for you as it is for my single friends out there. Be honest with yourself, as an individual and as a couple. Self-knowledge will help you see where you want to grow—where you are just surviving, and where you want to thrive.

Strive

For those of you who are single, I know that it can be easy to see singlehood as a curse. Whether you are 13, 16, 23, 31, or 51, time spent as a single (thanks to dating being one of the ultimate status symbol in our society) can be seen as something to wish away, hate, disdain, and even loathe. I know how scary, lonely, and anxiety-ridden it can be; but we know that those insecurities, fears, and doubts about yourself, your future, and especially who you're going to date can lead you down some dark roads—as in the Emoticoaster and the Cycle of Use.

I know it is not easy, but I hope you'll take a new and fresh look at this time in your life. Stop dwelling on everything you think you're not and on who you're not with, and focus on who you want to be and where you're going.

It is difficult to think of it this way, but the time you have before the altar, before the "I dos," is a gift. You have been given this time in your life to prepare and train. You won't need the Altar Switch (which doesn't exist anyway) because you have been training, growing, and forming yourself for the true Game of Life.

Women, how about this for your new motto: *"Strive to become the woman of your dreams, and you will attract the man of your dreams!"* Who is she? Who are you? By figuring out who you are and by knowing and going after *your* goals, hopes, and dreams, the man of your dreams will be attracted to *that* woman—not to who you wish you were, or who you used to be, and not who *he* wants you to be, but to the real *you!*

Men, every decision you make, every choice, big or small, is taking you closer or further away from the man you are truly called to be. So the real question is: "What kind of man are you striving to be?" Marriage may seem far off, or it may be on your doorstep, but it's best to begin with the end in mind. Who are you? Who do you want to be? When I ask men this question, and they think seriously about it, they almost always answer, "I want to be an amazing husband and father." If that is one of your goals in life, if you want to stand on the altar and be ready for your bride, you need to start preparing today to be strong, confident, and ready for true and authentic love and happiness. Sports and video games can have a place, but don't replace the real Game of Life with any other game.

I know what I am asking is not going to be easy, but nothing worth having in life ever is. And it's not going to happen overnight. Some Olympians train for years for a ten-second race. Musicians put in countless hours of practice for a two-hour performance. Blood, sweat, and tears are poured into sports and performances for trophies, medals, and stories to tell your grandkids someday. So, how hard are you willing to train to become the woman of your dreams, or the man you long to be? To what lengths are you willing to go and in what ways are you willing to sacrifice—right now—for your future spouse and family?

I hope that this book becomes a "page turner" in your life —a time when you turn the page and start a new chapter in life entitled *"Striving."* Out with the old and in with the new: Who do I want to be? What am I living for? Who am I living for? If you are called to marriage, your future spouse is out there; he or she does exist even if you may not be able to physically see him or her right now. The altar may be years away for you, but trust me—*striving* to become the woman of your dreams or *striving* to be the man you're called to be has to start today.

In order to train and prepare in the twenty-first century, we're going to need to be more than tough. We have to be *aware* and *prepare*. Attacks are coming hard and often. We have to be ready to fight back, and we have weapons, lots of them. In the next chapter, I want to introduce you to virtue, and to what I call *Emotional Virtue.*

6

WHAT IS EMOTIONAL VIRTUE?

It was a gorgeous spring day and I had taken the kids on a walk to the park. As I waited at the bottom of the slide for each kid to take their twentieth trip down, I noticed a young woman walking toward me. She had a shy look on her face, and as she got closer, I asked, "Hey, how's it going?" She smiled back and said, "I sure hope this doesn't freak you out, but I followed you here. I heard you speak a few months ago, and I just really need your help. Can we talk?"

She went on to tell me about her two-year relationship with her boyfriend that had just ended, her struggle to find friends, her fear of being alone, and the challenges she faced at school and at home with her family. She looked me and said:

> I know I struggle with the World's Idea of Perfect, and this breakup has caused me to doubt myself and really tear myself down. I am so tempted to jump on the Emoticoaster just to feel wanted or desired again, by any man. My emotions are running wild. I am so scared that I am going to be used again, and I don't want to use anyone, but I just feel so lost. I would give anything for a fresh start. I need a change. My eyes have been opened to what I *don't* want and what

I don't want to do, but Sarah, I don't know what I am supposed to do right now.

For years I have been hearing stories just like hers in countless conversations and in e-mails from women and men who are stuck in this similar spot. Every story is different—different situations, different people, different places—but at the center is the same kind of agonizing struggle.

As we try to navigate this life and relationships, especially the all-consuming anxiety of the 80-20 Problem's Big Three (Who am I going to date and eventually marry? What is he or she going to do for me and how is he or she going to make me feel? And how good can I look doing it?), we must strive to flip these three questions with Real Life's Big Three (Who do I want to be? What am I living for? And who am I living for?).

Virtue

We've already established the sobering reality that there is no Altar Switch, and becoming the person you're called to be doesn't just happen overnight. In the previous chapter, I pointed out that every choice you make, every decision, takes you one step closer or further away from the person you truly long to be. But what does living this out look like in your own head and heart, as well as in your relationships?

One answer, and one of our secret weapons (that I hope doesn't stay a secret any longer) is virtue. When applied to dating and relationships, I like to call it *Emotional Virtue*.

When I was in college, I had a professor ask our class, "What is virtue?" I remember thinking, "Patience is a virtue," and that was about as far as I got. As we dove deeper into what virtue was, my eyes were opened. What I learned went something like this:

Virtue is striving for human excellence.

Virtue is forming the habits of knowing and choosing the good.

Virtue harnesses and trains your passions and emotions to work toward the good.

Virtue gives you the freedom to love.

Wow. I would leave class shaking my head in disbelief —to think I was finally finding answers, answers that resonated deep within my mind and heart. As my professor laid this all out, I just couldn't get enough.

My thoughts, actions, and habits are forming who I am. Like it or not, the hard reality is that I am becoming a certain kind of person through the actions I take and the decisions I make in life. This all made sense to me. Reinforcing good habits (virtues) makes them stronger, and reinforcing bad habits (vices) likewise makes them stronger. And the stronger the good habits are reinforced, the freer I am to love. Therefore, my actions dictate who I am because each and every action helps to reinforce the person I am becoming. The question to ask then is not just, "What do I do right here and now?" but *Who do I want to be?* Since there is no Altar Switch, my actions in the present *are* connected to who I am becoming tomorrow and in the future.

This helps us to understand the quote about love from Chapter 4:

Love is not *primarily* a feeling, though it can be accompanied by feeling. That's the confusion of our time, confusing love's feeling with love itself. Love actually is a great act of the will. It's when I say, "I desire your good, not for my sake but for yours."

I remember thinking in the past: "I am free to love; free to love whom I desire; free to choose whom I love; free to choose how I love." But then I realized there is more to freedom than simply choosing what I want. There are other questions like: Am I *able?* Am I *capable* of loving in the full authentic way I want to? Am I *free* to do the good?

Think of a marathon runner preparing for a race. Now think about a person who has an intense desire to run a full marathon, but hasn't run around the block in over a year. Is the second runner truly free to run the marathon? Maybe. He is certainly free to put on those neon sneakers and matching neon sweatband and give it his all. But is he truly free to run the whole 26-mile race, without walking, and to finish it? Compare the "freedom" of the person who *wants* to run a marathon with the marathon runner who has been training and running every day for a year in preparation, miles upon miles for months, eating right, pushing himself to the limit, and building endurance. Most likely, the one who trains succeeds, while the other has just fallen prey to wishful thinking.

The runner who has prepared, trained, and sacrificed gains true freedom. Whether you are an athlete, a musician, a dancer, a writer, whatever your passion is, you know that it takes time to train and acquire the skill set necessary to carry out the task at hand. Blood, sweat, tears, long hours, and countless sacrifices go into mastering your craft. It is no different in the Game of Life. Virtues are the skills necessary to succeed in this most important of all games.

Attaining virtue—forming good habits, striving for excellence, developing the habit of doing the right thing, becoming more authentically free—just like mastering any craft, takes time and lots of discipline. It will be hard in the beginning. The marathon runner will feel every muscle screaming at him in his first training session; but over time, as he runs more and more miles, all of a sudden it doesn't hurt as much as it did in the beginning. Strength and endurance are built up, and then a ten-mile run *may actually feel good*; and perhaps even more shocking, after this pattern of training is established, a few days of not running may start to feel strange, like something is missing. So the training not only gives the person the ability to accomplish the task, but also the freedom to *enjoy* doing it, even though it was difficult in the beginning.

Emotional Virtue

As we have seen, our emotions and passions can play a huge part in the battle to attain virtue. Emotions and passions can get a bad rap sometimes. I know a lot of people who have it in their minds that emotions are bad—people who wish they weren't so emotional or passionate, or wish others in their lives weren't so emotional or passionate. Many people try to suppress or bottle up their emotions because of past experiences, or because they think the best way to handle their emotional life is to lock up their heart and throw away the key. But suppressing every emotion should never be the goal.

Here's the thing: emotions and passions are actually good! We have emotions and passions for a reason! They give life its zeal, its gusto. They are the fire that burns inside you, moving you to act and react—to help someone in need, to stand up against injustice, to love more fully. Emotions and passions stir your soul for a reason. You don't want to push them down, hide them, ignore them, or run from them. On the other hand, to take the other extreme, you don't want them to run wild and out of control, taking over your life. The trick is to learn to harness your emotions and direct them toward the good. We have to be the "boss of our thoughts," as I like to say, and not let the World's Idea of Perfect, the Emoticoaster, or the Cycle of Use set the agenda.

Emotions are good, but it is not their job to recognize the truth. Our mind must recognize truth; and in this task, it must not be dominated by our emotions. But once the mind is locked in on the truth, and our emotions are following our mind's lead, then we should *encourage* our emotions.

You have a head and a heart for a reason. Your mind has to be formed in what is true, good, and beautiful, so that your heart and will can act upon it. As said before, you can follow your heart sometimes, but don't forget to bring your head with you! Your emotions and passions have to be ordered toward living out virtue, making the virtuous decision, performing the virtuous act. Again, the goal is to order one's emotions—neither to suppress, nor to let them wildly take control.

Emotional Virtue, then, is *the right ordering of our thoughts, actions, and desires as they relate to our relationships*. This can be in anticipation of a future relationship, in the midst of one, or in dealing with the aftermath of one that has ended.

True Love and Authentic Relationships

If true love is not just a feeling (but may certainly be accompanied by feelings) then true love is also not just an emotion or a passion. Emotions and passions can be fleeting; they come and go. But if we buy into the lie that love is just a feeling, then our friendships, dating relationships, and marriages will only be as secure as the feelings upon which they are built; and when those "feelings" are gone, those relationships often dissolve.

This seems to mark the great divide: seeing love only as a feeling, as opposed to seeing love as an act of the will (based on the objective good and driven by virtue)—the divide between the World's Idea of Perfect and its Big Three and what I am proposing. In my experience, our lives and our relationships are enhanced when we put down the World's Idea of Perfect and pursue virtue in light of Real Life's Big Three, and treat love as a selfless regard for the good of the other. What we find is that when our relationships are based on a solid foundation, the *experience* of love actually grows all the richer. Feelings and emotions, rather than being bad, are taken to the next level when love is built on a sturdy framework. Living this out, externally and within our own hearts, is what *Emotional Virtue* is all about.

I am often asked, "If I emotionally enjoy the company of another or even the excitement of a budding relationship, does that mean I am using the other person emotionally?" No, of course not. We only need to keep in mind that our goal should be to anchor our emotional enjoyment in sincere love for the other—willing his or her good and always looking out for what is best for him or her.

There was a time when the only trait I knew to be a virtue was patience, but over the years I have come to know a few more. I have also come to find that when it comes to relationships, virtue is actually *very* attractive. In the next chapter, we will look at how women and men who are striving for virtue can turn a few heads—or, dare I say, may even be *Simply Irresistible*.

SIMPLY IRRESISTIBLE

Checklists. We are a people of checklists. We have lists of thousands of things to do in order to achieve success—whether it's fame, money, power, good looks, or admiration. Whether written down on a piece of paper with checkboxes beside them, saved in an app on your phone, or just flashing through your mind—these "checklists" are always reminding us of who we need to be; or perhaps more often, reminding us of everything we think we're not.

In the first chapter, The World's Idea of Perfect, we laid out a pretty good list of the world's expectations if we want to "make the team," or at least not be "invisible."

There is so much pressure to "have it all together"—to put on your "happy face," the "no, really, I'm fine" face. I hear it from college men, high school girls, mothers at our library's story time, high-powered businessmen, and pretty much everyone in between. The pressure to check off the boxes that lead to attaining the ultimate status symbols in our culture—success, fame, money, power, good looks, admiration—is all consuming.

A Different Checklist

We have already called out the World's Idea of Perfect, the Emoticoaster, and the Cycle of Use, but what about making up a checklist of our own for the Game of Life? Now, I'm not saying that people shouldn't strive to be successful in their career field, portray beauty in the way they dress, or provide well for their families. But maybe we should take a second look at the items on our checklist, especially those that often take up most of our mental energy.

Over the years, I have asked people, "What traits and characteristics do you find most attractive?" When I ask a group of men, they typically get into their "man huddle," arms draped around each other, swaying back in forth as they talk it over, and there is typically grunting. When I ask women, they practically pull out a four-page spreadsheet with color-coded columns and footnotes, with a slideshow, pictures, and videos to go with it.

As I compiled these lists from what the men and women had told me, two things became very clear: (1) the traits and characteristics that people described as attractive tended to be the fruit of living out the virtues (such as prudence, justice, courage, and temperance); (2) the lists looked very different from the world's checklists and its idea of "perfect." In fact, in striking contrast to the World's Idea of Perfect, the items on these lists are centered on the interior character of a person, not a person's exterior qualities. There are no numbers on a scale, specified pounds on the bench press, and not a single feature that could be Photoshopped.

Although these lists are certainly not exhaustive, and more could certainly be added, they are a great place to start.

A summary of the list that the guys made for what they are looking for in a woman looks like this:

The Simply Irresistible Virtuous Woman		
Feminine	Confident	Committed
Gentle and kind	Stands up for what is right and seeks the truth	Her relationship with God comes first in her life
Graceful and sincere	Has courage, is not afraid to confront and help someone	Puts others first, before herself
Patient and flexible	Genuinely excited for another, not jealous or vain	Strives for excellence in all things: in chastity, in sobriety, and tries her hardest in academics or her career
Doesn't gossip, isn't rude	Speaks with conviction	Not led solely by her emotions and passions
Tries to eliminate drama, not create it	Responsible	Maintains balance and order in life
Poised and modest	Prudent	Lives a life of charity and service
Open to the needs of others	Humble and honest	Forgiving
Nurturing and welcoming	Secure	Trustworthy and loyal
Joyful and fun	Sensitive to the needs of others	Pure

The women out there are probably thinking, "Whoa, baby! Sarah, that is a pretty tall order!" Yes, it is, but before you write it off, take a deep breath and say this out loud: "Striving, striving—*not perfect*—but striving." The woman who is striving to live out the virtues on this list is *Simply Irresistible*. You will not find a woman walking the earth who perfectly embodies all these traits and characteristics. So, men, you can stop waiting for her, or expecting your girlfriend or wife to be perfect. That woman does not exist. What you are looking for is a woman who is striving.

Ladies, I promise you, I have heard it from man after man: "A woman who knows and cares about these characteristics and is striving for virtue is *truly* so attractive." This list is not just for the single ladies out there! It's for everybody—13, 16, 23, 31, or 51, for any and every stage of life. Virtue brings joy, peace, and beauty to one's life. Virtue and striving for virtue is certainly not something you do just to "get a man." No, it is a lifelong journey toward living out authentic love and pursuing happiness. But still, it is what people find genuinely attractive in others. Can you imagine the joy of having friends and families built around living out and fostering these characteristics and traits?

Here's the list that the women made for what they are looking for in a man:

The Simply Irresistible Virtuous Man		
Masculine	Confident	Committed
Leader	Stands up for what is right and seeks the truth	His relationship with God comes first in his life
Provider	Has courage, is not afraid to confront and help someone	Puts others first, before himself
Protector	Genuinely excited for another, not jealous or vain	Strives for excellence in all things: in chastity, in sobriety, and tries his hardest in academics or his career
Initiator	Speaks with conviction	Not led solely by his emotions or passions
Chivalrous	Responsible	Maintains balance and order in life
Brave and courageous	Prudent	Lives a life of charity and service
Gentle and respectful	Humble and honest	Forgiving
Intuitive and patient	Secure	Trustworthy and loyal
Joyful and fun	Sensitive to the needs of others	Pure

Gentlemen, I promise you, I have heard it from woman after woman: "A man who cares about these characteristics and is striving for virtue is *truly* so attractive." And just like the Simply Irresistible Virtuous Woman's list, it is not just for single men! There are countless husbands, fathers, and other strong men who are striving for these virtues in their lives! Ladies, please remember, you will not find a man walking the earth who perfectly exemplifies all these traits and characteristics, so you can stop waiting for him, or expecting your boyfriend or husband to be perfect. That man does not exist. Once again, what you are looking for is a man who is striving.

Did you notice that I had to make sure that both sexes knew that the opposite sex told me that these lists *are* what they find attractive? That was for a reason. When I give talks around the country, there is typically one woman (or twenty) who tell me, "There are no good guys! No good guys anywhere—none. I am going to die alone with a hundred cats!" And there is usually a group of guys who pull me aside and whisper, "Are you sure that this is what the girls want? If this is what they want, then why do they throw themselves at guys who are the complete opposite?"

Stereotypes and Brokenness

The stereotype that men are "only concerned with sex and don't care about women or relationships and really only care about themselves" is out there. So is the stereotype that women are "needy, overly emotional, high-maintenance 'takers' who only care about themselves." These are boxes that people put each other in, either based on the wounds of past relationships, or because of the sad reality of brokenness playing out in the present. But I have to be honest with you—after countless conversations, it's clear that most men and women don't really want to be either stereotype.

As we mentioned, the world likes to mess with us. But now that we have access to the truth about virtue and Emotional Virtue, my hope is that these new ideas of what is true, good, and beautiful—what is truly attractive and simply irresistible—can begin to form and transform your way of thinking and untwist some of the lies and pressures you have felt in the past.

Let's take a closer look at the *Simply Irresistible* lists; I'm sure as you were reading through them, there may have been a few items where you could say to yourself, "Oh, yeah, I'm good there." Or, "I don't struggle too much with that one." But if you are like me, as you read through the list, there were also a few that felt like a jab to the heart and to the ego.

Part of striving for and living out virtue is understanding that you are not perfect, and that at points you will fail. We all have an intense fear of failure. It is in our human nature to want to impress, and we all desire praise and admiration. This goes hand in hand with the pressure to "have it all together," and there is no rest in this quest for perfection.

It is amazing to see how fast someone will move to take down what they think is a terrible picture of themselves on social media, or to hear the lies people will tell in order to keep up their image, or the people they will walk on in order to "stay on top of the pack."

But what do you do when you're faced with failure? What do you do when you've fallen off the horse, face down, not able to get up—when a dating relationship doesn't work out, a group of friends drops you, fears plague you and cause you to doubt your self-worth? What do you do when insecurities stab at you and cause you to spiral into despair, into depression, anxiety, eating disorders, cutting, addictions, handing your body over to be used, or using someone else to take away the pain?

We all have our struggles, our pasts, our wounds, our mistakes, and our failures. We've seen how the world tries to mess with us, with its plans and checklists. But now we have a new awareness—the weapons of virtue, Emotional Virtue, truth, goodness, beauty, and the Simply Irresistible lists to fight back with. Yet even with all these weapons, if we're really going to figure out this whole Game of Life and relationships, there is still more left to do, and so the next stop on our journey is to *Lay It All Down*.

8

LAY IT ALL DOWN

One night a group of college students and I were devouring a triple batch of cookie dough around my kitchen island while we hashed out life—the good, the bad, and the ugly. Then one girl pointed her spoon straight at me and asked, "Sarah, did you ever struggle with any of this?" All the eyes around the table were fixed on me, and I smiled with a very genuine understanding of exactly what they were getting at.

I grew up in an amazing family with the most loving Mom, Dad, and brothers, but even with the wonderful childhood and family I was blessed with, like I said before, no one gets out of junior high, high school, and college completely unscathed.

Gosh, did I *ever* feel the pressure of the World's Idea of Perfect, as I made the checklists in my head (and some on paper). I fell prey to versions of what I now call the Emoticoaster, and the Cycle of Use certainly left me with my share of wounds. I was definitely confused about what true love was, and I wore different masks to hide the pain and emptiness. I often felt the effects of competition and comparing, insecurities about my image, and especially my body image, seemed to weigh me down. I guess now you know why it is so easy for me to write about all this, and why I'll do anything to help.

Answers came during a low point in my life, early in college. I was doubting my worth and whether I was ever going to find (or deserve) "the one." Like many who are single, so much of my anxiety centered around dating and relationships. I felt like I was working my tail off to be the "perfect" dating material, but I was losing patience and growing bitter with men, myself, and even God. My mind and heart were consumed with this dilemma that seemed to touch every corner and recess of my very existence. Life felt heavy and I was tired of carrying the load.

Running

Searching for direction, I signed up for a retreat. That weekend, to my surprise, I found myself going to confession with a young priest, and after I poured my heart out to him, he gave me some advice that would radically change the way I viewed dating—and even the way I viewed my life. Here is what he said:

> I want you to run, run to Jesus, and I want you to take everything you are feeling, everything you are worried about, your past, your pain, and I want you to lay it all down at His feet. Put everything in a box and drop it off at His feet. You don't have to carry it anymore. Fall into His arms and let Him love you and forgive you; and when you are strong, and whole, and you have been healing, I want you to run *with* Him; and when the time is right, glance to the side and see who is running with you.

It felt like a ton of bricks had fallen from my shoulders. Not only had I been chasing after guys, trying to get their attention, trying to mold them into exactly what I wanted them to be, dragging them, spinning them around on the Emoticoaster until I made us both sick—but I had also lost sight of the goal. I had taken my eyes off the prize. I was so distracted and concerned about what some guy was going to do for me—what I needed from him to make me whole, what I had to have in order to mask the insecurities I tried so desperately to hide—that I had lost sight of the true meaning of my life.

I had started to despair, and it was wreaking havoc on my mind, heart, and especially my thoughts and emotions. But this new idea that was presented to me, for some reason brought an incredible sense of relief. I dared to ask, "You mean I can stop? You're giving me permission to stop? You honestly think it would be a good idea to *Lay It All Down*—to stop worrying, stop scheming, stop comparing, stop manipulating, and even to stop despairing?"

A flood of relief washed over me—after years of restlessness and fear, feeling like my soul was trapped, like I was pushing on a pull door—you know, when you are trying to get out of a building and you are pushing, throwing your whole body into a door to try to get it to open. You pound the door with your fist, and notice that you just punched a sticker with four little letters saying "PULL." You step back, grab the door handle, pull, and effortlessly open the door, amazed that you didn't think to just read the sign.

But it was as clear as the PULL sign on the door. RUN. Not into the arms of a man, not away from my problems, but toward our Lord. I don't know where you are in your relationship with God; you may be very close to Him, or He may seem very far away; or you may be in a similar place as I was.

Surrender

Up until that time, I had sidelined God. In my mind, He was "there," but only in a way that I was comfortable with. I was comfortable with God in my life as a mix of cheerleader/ATM machine/teddy bear/genie in a bottle. But I can't begin to describe my relief at the idea of laying it all down at His feet, giving my problems to Someone who could actually do something about them—and no longer putting on a mask, but learning how to truly be myself, to start anew, to heal, grow, and run. I knew this was going to require some action and work, but my heart ached for it, and for the first time in a long while I felt a tinge of excitement:

Run to Jesus, and fall into His arms.

Run toward our Lord and live for Him.

Run the race of life, the Game of Life, with Him.

I had to surrender; I had to wave the white flag—not in defeat, but in *victory*. For the first time in my life, I realized that I couldn't do this on my own. But what was more amazing was the understanding that I didn't *have to* do it all on my own—and even that I wasn't *supposed to* do it all on my own. I finally grasped the truth that I had to surrender my life to the One, the only One who could truly give me everything my heart desired. I had to give my heart to the only One who could put the pieces back together, the One who could comfort me, love me, accept me, forgive me, and give me permission to forgive myself. I was not lost, hope was not lost. I was not abandoned— I was loved.

Healing and the Search for Happiness

Part of keeping God on the sidelines was so that I could keep Him at a distance; I was so scared of letting anyone see my fears and failings. I worked so hard to keep them secret and hidden that I even tried to hide them from God. How could anyone love me? Love my flaws, my past? I thought it was impossible. No matter how hard I tried, or even tried to fake it, I truly believed that even God couldn't love my weaknesses, mistakes, and imperfections.

I couldn't have been more wrong. It was actually the exact opposite. I felt like I had to prove myself to God, just like I felt I had to prove myself to everyone else. I would say to myself, "Okay, I need to fix that, change that, stop that, lose ten pounds, and then I will present myself to God—the perfect Sarah—and *then* He will love me."

My thinking was so wrong. It was backward. God wants you to come to Him, with all your fears, all your insecurities, all your weaknesses and wounds, your past, all of you. You don't have to hide from Him. Run to Him; drop everything off at His feet and let Him comfort you, tell you how proud of you He is, how He wants to forgive you, build you up and bring you healing and peace.

Jesus desires to love you like no human being can. He has given man and woman to each other to be a sign of His love, but that love doesn't replace our need for His love. In the same way, no man or woman can be your Savior; and trying to make someone your Savior can actually ruin the relationship. It's not possible; no one is capable of being "your everything" or being your god. It's too heavy of a burden; your significant other will break under the weight and pressure, and when they inevitably fall short, you will be disappointed.

It can be easy to seek to fulfill our desires with anything other than God. Every decision you made in the past (whether it turned out well, or in the end was a complete disaster) was made because you believed that decision would truly make you happy, and fulfill a desire you longed for.

When you made any such decision, it may have seemed like the right thing to do at the time, as if it would ultimately fulfill you. But whether those decisions led to the pain of an unbearable breakup, being rejected, overlooked, abused, used, or facing the reality that you have used or hurt someone else—deep down, those choices were really a search for God, though you may not have recognized it at the time. We all desire infinite happiness (a desire that drives all our decisions) and this desire can only find fulfillment in God Himself.

You may have fallen into a dark time and lost your virginity; you may have given it away, or you may have had your virginity taken from you. You may feel as though you have been stripped emotionally. You may have fallen into struggles with alcohol, drugs, pornography, sexual sin, eating disorders, cutting, depression, or anxiety. You may have made decisions in life that you believed would truly make you happy but that hurt you in the end.

So many people are secretly and silently suffering from the wounds and heaviness of life and with the aftermath of decisions they've made; and many think that they are alone, that they are the only ones struggling with this type of pain from the past or temptations in the present. I see this play out so often in the battle against pornography and sexual sin fought by both men and women. Many men have told me that fighting this temptation is the hardest thing they have to endure in their lives. And though many people are aware of men's battle with pornography, I also hear from many women about their struggles with pornography and sexual sin as well. Whether it was their own curiosity, or they were exposed to porn by friends or a boyfriend, or were swept up by erotic romance novels, movies, or steamy online relationships, the shame and embarrassment they feel is truly unbearable; and because it is not talked about often, many women believe that they face this trial alone.

It can be easy to believe that your desire for love, acceptance, admiration, comfort, or pleasure can be fulfilled emotionally or sexually. But when that desire isn't ordered toward true love and what is truly best for the beloved in your life (or those who will be in your life someday—your future spouse and children), we end up using others, and trying to fill the infinite desire of our heart with something finite, something other than God.

As with my experience, the pain and shame of past mistakes is one of the main reasons men and women keep God at a distance. They don't believe that God (or anyone else for that matter) could forgive them for their past, their mistakes, or their struggles. Forgiving others and asking for forgiveness from others, accepting forgiveness from God, and forgiving yourself are some of the hardest things to do in life. But Jesus is waiting for you, with arms wide open, and ready to take away all the pain of your past that you have now placed in that box and put at His feet. He is waiting to embrace you and free you from the chains that hold you down and hold you back from true love. He is waiting for you to experience true love from Him, true love from others, and the ability to see your true identity, dignity, and worth through *His* eyes.

The wounds of the past that have stacked up over time did not get there overnight, and so this healing will take time. But I promise you, His mercy, forgiveness, grace, and love is waiting for you every single time you stumble and fall—and *especially* when you fall.

I want you to live this life to the fullest and wring out every ounce of joy and happiness. Based on my experience, I promise you that running to the Lord, laying it all down, and running the race of life with *Him* will not disappoint you.

A New Start

Many people have made commitments to save themselves for their future spouses. Countless people have recommitted themselves to wait until their wedding night to give all of themselves to their spouse, and you can, too. Some people sign commitment cards or write a letter to God. Many people write letters to their future spouses, telling them of their commitment. I love this. Pray for your future spouse, write letters to him or her while you are preparing for that day at the altar. Put all those passions and emotions you are feeling in writing for him or her; don't waste them on the Emoticoaster. On your wedding day, your spouse will love to read about how hard you worked, how patiently you waited, and how great your love was even before the two of you ever met.

Trust me, in knowing and talking with the men and women who have made this commitment or recommitment, and from my own personal experience, no matter what things have looked like in your past, over time and with God's help your open and painful wounds really do heal.

I don't know where you are in your relationship with God, but I am asking you to give God a chance. Give God a chance to love you. Life won't always be easy. You will fail—you will fall, you will have bad days or bad years. But always trust that you can turn to Him; His mercy and love will always welcome you with open arms, *every single time*. Through prayer, confession, Scripture, the sacraments, and countless other ways, we can come to know and experience His love and grace. That amazing advice I was given that day in college really did change my perspective—not only on dating, but on life:

> I want you to run, run to Jesus, and I want you to take everything you are feeling, everything you are worried about, your past, your pain, and I want you to lay it all down at His feet. Put everything in a box and drop it off at His feet. You don't have to carry it anymore. Fall into His arms and let Him love you and forgive you; and when you are strong, and whole, and you have been healing, I want you to run *with* Him; and when the time is right, glance to the side and see who is running with you.

Take a deep breath. I pray you are soaking in a new reality, a new perspective, and I hope you have a tinge of excitement running through your veins. We've called out the attacks and put them in their place. We've decided there has to be a better way to fight them and we've answered them with virtue—not just being virtuous in order to check off boxes and be successful, but living a full life, a life where virtue flows out of and is ordered to *love for God and others*. The invitation to lay it all down at His feet and let faith, mercy, love, and peace enter our hearts and lives is our first step toward not just healing, but also to a much richer and happier life.

Now that we've laid this solid foundation, we're ready to take on the question of relationships. If you are single, you are probably thinking: "Please, Lord, now that I'm healing and running, when the time is right and I glance over, could you point out my significant other with a flash of lightning or have him or her light up in fluorescent yellow so I know they are 'the one'? Please, Lord!"

I wish that was how it worked. Boy, wouldn't that make things a lot easier! In the third part of this book, I want to take everything we've built up and apply it to contemporary relationships. In case you haven't noticed, dating can be a scary, confusing, crazy mess sometimes! But we have already done the "heavy lifting" and we're ready to run. I know you're probably thinking, "Let's figure out how to get to the part where I see who's running with me!" And that's exactly where we'll start. But when you first glance, it might not be exactly who you were expecting.

A ROADMAP WITH
THE END IN MIND

9

FINDING YOUR POSSE

With the new plan of running the race of life with our Lord, and when the time is right, to glance to the side and see who is running with you, I know that you may be hoping to look over and see some ridiculously good looking, faithful, virtue-driven member of the opposite sex—and if that is who you see, great. But first, I hope you see your *posse*, that group of like-minded friends running the race with you.

I know twenty-first-century dating relationships are complicated, but I think finding a solid group of friends nowadays may be just as hard! But nothing, and I mean nothing, could be more vital to figuring out this whole Game of Life than finding good friends—friends who are calling you to greatness and encouraging you to become the very best you can be. And making good friends is also a very important step on the road to preparing for your relationship with Mr. or Mrs. Right.

As we talked about in the first part of this book, the bullying of junior high, the "who's talking to who" of high school, and the dog-eat-dog world of college and beyond make it such a struggle to trust anyone these days. It is definitely hard to trust the opposite sex; but trusting members of the same sex can be just as challenging. And who can blame people? Life is full of gossip, name-dropping, one-upping, backstabbing, rumors and lies, cheating, and the drama that flows from it all. Popularity contests, comparing, and competing are at an all-time high. Friends can become enemies in the blink of an eye—or in the "ding" of a text or post.

You have probably figured out by now that I am a really big fan of a drama-free life. All the drama I just mentioned is exhausting, so I don't think we need to add to it or make it any worse.

So how do we lay this groundwork for dating relationships? How do women find their posse of other amazing women to run with? And how do men rally together with their band of brothers and take on this Game of Life?

If you are a woman, you *know* how hard it is to be a woman. The first thing I would like you to do is to make this pledge with me: *From this day forward, through my words and actions, I will try never to make life harder on another woman.*

And if you are a man, you *know* how hard it is to be a man, so I ask you to make this commitment: *From this day forward, through my words and actions, I will try never to make life harder on another man.*

I think that is a good place to start. We have to have each other's backs. We have to protect and respect one another, both our friends of the same sex and those of the opposite sex. We truly need each other and have to look out for one another.

You will need friends to go to when the world gets loud, to reassure you of your worth when you doubt, to support you through struggles and hard times which will inevitably come your way. You will need your posse by your side as you strive for virtue. So, think of these great friends as "workout partners" in the Game of Life, running beside you toward our Lord, challenging you to a higher standard and ready to pick you up when you fall.

I have found this type of accountability and support to be extremely important in the Game of Life. It is one thing to make goals, define your roles, and list what virtues you need to work on; but taking those lists and sharing them with friends and family can take you to a whole new level.

Including your family on this journey may be natural for some and very difficult for others. You may have a great relationship with your family, and they may also be some of your closest friends, or you may have a family situation that has been the cause of great pain and struggle in your life. I pray that this book helps you in your journey with your family as well as with your friends—whether it is healing, forgiveness, growing in virtue, or learning how to love and be loved by your family. I pray that your family can be a great source of strength and love for you in your life.

The Virtue Challenge

Many people take my *Virtue Challenge* together. It goes like this: every week you pick a virtue (you can use the Simply Irresistible lists or any other list of virtues to get you started) and write that virtue down. Under the virtue, you list three practical, realistic, and concrete ways that you are going to grow in that virtue during the week. Beside it, you also list three obstacles that could stand in your way, so that you are ready for them and have a prior awareness of how they might affect you.

Although you can certainly do this on your own, I recommend sharing it with a trustworthy friend, family member, or posse; again, having this accountability and encouragement is powerful. Throughout the week, you can support each other and be there for one another. It is also important for you to see your friends working on different virtues, training for the Game of Life right alongside you. Friends who share life together in this way often forge bonds that can last a lifetime.

Before you go to bed each night, evaluate your day: How did you live out the virtue you are working on? What obstacles stood in the way, and how did you fight back? What do you want to do tomorrow in order to grow in that virtue? At the end of the week, get together with your friend or posse and share how the week went. Be honest, talk it out, and then pick your new virtue to work on in the upcoming week. You may find yourself picking the same virtue over and over again, and that's okay. Just like the marathon runner we talked about earlier, it will be hard in the beginning; but over time, and with hard work and perseverance, you will be amazed by how far you've come!

There is a posse of men I know who really exemplify the strength and perseverance of living out the Virtue Challenge together. They confided in me that all five of them were fighting addictions to pornography and sexual sin. They got together and talked about it openly and honestly and decided to hold each other accountable: If any one of the guys fell in a moment of weakness, he would send out a group text to all the men in the posse, and from that moment on all five men would fast for twenty-four hours. No one ate. They prayed for each other and sacrificed eating for *twenty-four hours*.

Talk about accountability! They told me that in the beginning it was difficult, very difficult. But what was beautiful about it was that when a guy was tempted, he had to ask himself, "If I do this, if I watch this or look at that, and commit sexual sin, I will be causing my friends (and myself) to go without eating for twenty-four hours. Is that what I want to do? Is it worth it?"

One guy told me that within days he had deleted or thrown away almost all his usual pornography "go-tos." He said, "I would be tempted and then the reality of sending that text and causing all my closest friends to suffer would kick in, and I would say to myself, 'I've got to get out of here.' Then I would usually call up a friend and we would go hang out and do something together. Sometimes we'd even go pig out at a Chinese buffet!"

I can't tell you how much I respect that posse of men, and how proud of them I am. Hearing stories like theirs and countless others of how groups of friends have used the Virtue Challenge in many unique ways to fight different temptations and struggles is truly amazing, and I am so inspired by all of them.

Steps to Finding Your Posse

You may already have a solid group of friends of the same sex. Thank God for them and start running the race of life together. Don't be exclusive—invite new friends to run with you! But my guess is that most of you are probably thinking, "Right, Sarah, and just where am I going to find these friends?" I know, and don't think for a moment that I think this is easy. I was bullied so badly in junior high that I had to switch schools. I know how hard it is, but I know that the effort is more than worth it.

For starters, I've put together the *Five Steps to Finding Your Posse*:

1) *Have courage.* I need you to muster up the virtue of courage and step out of your comfort zone a bit. Don't let fears or events of the past paralyze you; don't negatively project the past upon the future. Have courage and confidence to take what you are learning, share it, and find people who want to run with you.

2) *Set your priorities.* In light of all we've said, you need to reevaluate what you value in a friend. Surround yourself with people who are positive and lift you up and don't bring you down. I love the well-known quote, "Show me your five closest friends and I'll show you your future." Friends can bring out the best in you or they can bring out the worst in you. If your new priorities in life are God, virtue, truth, service and love, then surround yourself with friends who have the same priorities. What often happens is that people who might not seem to be the same "type" can actually become amazing friends when their lives are ordered toward the same goal. It's remarkable how people who may appear to be a little different on the outside can come together when their lives are centered on virtue and running toward our Lord—they often become lifelong friends. Give people a chance. Remember, your friends don't have to measure up to the World's Idea of Perfect.

3) *Be vulnerable.* Human beings have a fear of failure. It is very hard for us to reveal our shortcomings and struggles, but part of running with your posse and with our Lord is admitting that you're not perfect, admitting that you're human! Don't be satisfied with shallow conversations about nothing. Don't be satisfied with a shallow life about nothing. Pursue the true, the good, and the beautiful together. Be honest about life and about your virtues and struggles; encourage one another and be real with one

another. This creates an environment of trust, safety, and support.

4) *Reach out.* All of us have probably experienced what it feels like to be alone. Even with a large entourage around all the time, many can still feel very alone. Look for others who may be struggling or going through a hard time. Look for people who may be trying to break free from the Cycle of Use and could really use a virtuous, listening ear. I know of many "Hey, how are you doing?" conversations that have led to deep friendships over time. By the way, genuinely reaching out to others in need pretty much covers half of the Simply Irresistible lists!

5) *Pray for good friends.* Never underestimate the power of prayer. After I was bullied in junior high, I started asking God to put friends in my life who loved and supported me. Be patient and trust; it might not happen right away, but God does hear you. I eventually found my posse, and I know it was an answered prayer.

So imagine this: we have an amazing posse of women who are growing in courage, setting new priorities for their lives, being authentic, real, and vulnerable with each other, and reaching out to others. Sounds great, right? Then suppose we have an amazing posse of men who are likewise growing in courage and virtue as men, setting virtue-driven priorities, having real conversations, and being vulnerable with one another, all the while reaching out and getting out of their comfort zones. Both the men and women are striving to emulate their Simply Irresistible lists and encouraging one another and looking out for one another. *Now, please, male posse and female posse, spend time together!* Note, this should not be a "flirtfest," where everyone just pretends like they're dating. No, these are people striving for virtue, having fun, sharing life, and making memories with other virtuous people! Some of my greatest memories from high school and college took place in this kind of setting.

Virtuous Friends and the Ultimate Goal

Remember, this is supposed to be a drama-free zone. One way to preserve such an amazing and healthy environment is to keep in mind what we said about the 80-20 Problem and Its Big Three, and try to flip it with our Real Life's Big Three: (1) Who do I want to be? (2) What am I living for? (3) Who am I living for? If your posse's conversations can be directed toward Real Life's Big Three and away from the 80-20's Big Three, then it will help keep the whole group moving toward the true goal of our lives—running to our Lord, growing in virtue, and doing so with joy and love.

I know that this can all be a huge challenge in the "pressure to date and have a boyfriend/girlfriend" culture we live in, but it will go a long way if you can see the opposite sex first as friends, not just great dating material. Remember the importance of seeing love as a great act of the will, not just a feeling. Remember Emotional Virtue—applying virtue to our emotions and passions as it pertains to relationships. This is an awesome setting to practice forming your mind and seeing the opposite sex as they truly are: fellow friends on the journey, friends with great dignity who are never to be used, but to be protected and respected. Your goal should be to love them in the truest sense of the word, to will their good and help them reach their ultimate goal.

Also, finding your posse of women or posse of men and then spending time with friends of the opposite sex is one of the greatest things you can do to build up your confidence. Having friends who build you up—encourage you, support you, and allow you to be you—is priceless.

Here's how one woman expressed the freedom she discovered by doing this:

> The "perfect recipe" for getting the best boyfriend is getting to know myself, my values, and doing what makes me happy and joyful and being in the "right circles of people" (going to places where people with similar values and interests are most likely to go). I call it the "perfect recipe" cause it's a win-win, no matter what happens. If I find my soulmate, my future husband—that's great. But if I don't find him, I end up doing what I love to do and what makes me happy, which is also awesome, so I win no matter what happens!

Let time and trust build these friendships. I know it is tempting to start looking at your guy friends or female friends as potential significant others, but really savor this time that you have to work on authentic friendships. Many say they want to marry their best friend. Well, the roots of that friendship have to start somewhere.

Ladies, I like this quote: "Dance with God, and He will let the perfect man cut in." But I've altered it a bit, and I think I like my quote even better: "Dance with God, and trust that He will let the man He's chosen for you join in!" Don't run around the dance floor throwing yourself at guys, trying to fill the void. But don't stand there like a wallflower feeling sorry for yourself either. Dance with God, and get better at dancing, so you're ready for the partner that God taps and has prepared just for you!

For the gentlemen: "Strength train with our Lord, play the Game of Life, and use His life as your example of how to love." It's not going to be easy to deny yourself and fight temptation, to stand up for what is right, and not just live for yourself. Consider this: the Cross of Christ is forever a symbol and icon of true love; can there be a more manly expression of love and sacrifice than that? Champions are made by doing the little things, and the war is won in the small battles of life. Being faithful and committed in the small things leads to heroic virtue when it truly counts. Indeed, it is in doing the little things *now* that you develop the character to become that husband and father you hope to be someday.

Women, let the men be men. Let them practice chivalry, for example, by holding the door open for you and allowing them to anticipate your needs. Give them the opportunity to serve, for a man desires to look after a woman in friendship and respect. Don't instantly jump to the conclusion that acting like a gentleman equals hitting on you; they are not the same thing. Men confide in me all the time that they worry that their polite gestures are taken to mean more, putting them in awkward situations and discouraging them from practicing these very virtues. Gentlemen, thank you for serving—serving, not just flirting. Women are sensitive to flirtation, so if you serve one woman, make sure you try to serve them all—not just the ones you may be attracted to.

Remember, we all have a choice: a choice to help each other along this journey, to protect and respect one another, or a choice to hurt one another. In big and small ways, I pray you have learned some "secrets" about the opposite sex and how they work. The importance of building authentic friendships is one of the most important principles I hope you take from this book; it may also be one of the most important things you can do to lay a foundation for authentic dating relationships in the future. My prayer is that you find your posse and perhaps read this book together, using it as a guide to focus the whole group on what matters most and strive to live it out together.

In the next chapter, we will dive deeper into the ways that men and women can either help or hurt each other and take a closer look at what Emotional Virtue looks like in healthy interactions between the sexes. We will see that getting our true intentions rightly aligned plays a most important role. Just please, *Don't Shoot the Messenger*.

DON'T SHOOT THE MESSENGER: MODESTY OF INTENTIONS

Within a two-week period, I had two separate discussions that opened my eyes to a conversation that appears not to be happening between men and women. The first one went like this:

"Hey, Sarah, can I ask you a question?" a young woman asked me.

"Sure," I replied.

"So, I've been talking to this guy for about six months, and we text a lot. He'll flirt with me, and we hang out sometimes, but I just can't figure out where we stand. I think he likes me, but then sometimes he ignores me in public, or in a group—and then the minute I'm back in my room, he texts me. I think there's something more between us, I think we're kind of dating, but I don't know. What should I do?"

I answered, "I think you should probably talk to him about how you are feeling, and open the door to see where he stands. You can't live in emotional limbo anymore. Six months is a long time."

"I know you're right. Okay, thanks, Sarah. I'll let you know how it goes!" She gave me a quick hug and a smile and off she went.

A few days later, she came back, shoulders slumped and a look of sadness in her eyes. "How did it go?" I gently inquired.

She looked at me and said, "I opened up about every-thing and asked him where we stood and how he felt about me, and he said, 'Oh, whoa, we're just friends. If you can't control yourself, that's your own problem.'" Wow. My jaw practically hit the floor. Here was this beautiful woman, who had thought a relationship was going somewhere, only to find that she had been wrapped up in a web that left her confused, questioning her self-worth, and probably burdened with six months of emotional baggage. My heart ached for her.

Not two weeks later, a guy pulled me aside and said, "Hey, Sarah, can I talk to you?"

"Sure," I replied.

"Okay, here's the deal," he started in. "There's this girl friend of mine, not girlfriend, a female friend of mine, who is just awesome. She is funny, smart, and beautiful. But sometimes she wears really low-cut tops, and really short skirts, and I feel like I'm trying to focus on her from the neck up so that I don't think about using her from the neck down. I don't want anyone to use her like that. What do I do?"

"Maybe you could talk to her?" I suggested.

He looked at me like I had just asked him to try to eat his arm off. "Noooo," he moaned. "Can you talk to her, Sarah?"

"I could," I answered, "but I think it will mean a lot more coming from you."

He looked at me again. "Noooo," he replied. Then he went on, "Maybe you're right, but what the heck do I say?"

So we came up with a plan. He wrote out a script and was excited to practice.

"Come back and let me know how it goes," I yelled as he jogged away.

A few days later, he came back to me. I could sense his feeling of defeat. "How did it go?" I asked softly.

"I told her everything—how she was pretty, smart, funny, and that I didn't want anyone to use her body, and she looked at me and said, 'Look, if you can't control yourself, that's your own problem.'" I stood there dumbfounded. Not so much at her reaction, which is unfortunately fairly common, but at the sound of the exact same words I'd heard just a few weeks before: *"If you can't control yourself, that's your own problem."*

Helping, Hurting, and Understanding

I listen to story after story that are just like these two encounters. Although men and women are similar in many ways, they are also different, and have different struggles. In order to see how our choice to help or to hurt each other does affect the opposite sex, we have to look at how men and women struggle differently.

Sometimes I feel as though I hold the hand of the women in one hand and the hand of the men in the other, and I am the messenger. I look to the men and say, "Listen, when you flirt, text, show women emotionally saturated attention, give all kinds of signs that you are interested in something more, and then completely drop them, it does crazy things to their head and heart. You can really hurt them."

And then I turn to the women and say, "Listen, the men are fighting an unbelievable battle against the world telling them that women are *just* their bodies, that it's okay to use women as objects of sexual gratification; they're fighting pornography and sexual sin, and when you dress half-naked, it does crazy things to their head and heart. You can really hurt them."

These struggles probably don't come as a surprise to the men or the women, but I am told that even though the opposite sex may have heard these things before, it is hard for them to truly grasp the *degree* and *intensity* of the struggle.

Women beg me to tell men how hard it is on them when men flirt, snuggle, cuddle, text, text, and text some more. Women already struggle with mental stalking, and when a guy brushes his shoulder up against hers, she can jump from, "Hi, what's your name?" to the marriage proposal in less than three seconds. And then men beg me to tell the women how hard it is to keep their minds pure; they want to respect women and love them the way they should be loved, but lots of skin, sensual and suggestive body language, and flirtation sends their thoughts straight to "the sexual" in less than three seconds.

This is where I beg you, please, *Don't Shoot the Messenger!* I come to you in the name of the opposite sex, with the desire for love, peace, and understanding. I come in the name of virtue, especially Emotional Virtue, and as a fierce opponent of the Cycle of Use—so, please, don't shoot the messenger!

No one wants to be told what to wear or how to act —especially me, a woman, telling other women how to dress. No, thank you, I value my life. Okay, I'm being a bit sarcastic, but ladies, you know I'm right. Or me, a woman, telling men how to act could be difficult. But this conversation between the sexes needs to happen, so here we go.

For the Gentlemen

At first glance, Emotional Virtue may come across as more of a feminine phrase or girl problem, but in reality, it is exactly what a lot of men need to be aware of. Applying virtue to the way you emotionally interact with women is very important. Think back to the frat boys who told me how they sought to "get game" by emotionally manipulating women to obtain physical gratification. You may not be a slick frat boy, but whether you realize it or not, many men are exploiting women's emotional sensitivity and vulnerability for their own gain, whether that gain on the part of the men is physical or emotional.

Men will often have two, six, or even ten women in their cell phone who they text, or are "talking" to. Just like the story at the beginning of this chapter, there are women strung out all over the country who have been emotionally wounded by the ambiguity and lack of commitment from men. And texting is killing commitment and authentic conversation—because texting is a very *noncommittal* way to flirt. Men admit to me that texting is safer, a crutch, a way to avoid rejection. But having multiple women on "standby" wreaks havoc on women, hurting their self-confidence and creating all kinds of doubt and confusion.

The Cell Phone Challenge

One practical way the men can help women is by taking my *Cell Phone Challenge.* Men (and many women also) have committed to the Cell Phone Challenge in order to bring about an awareness and a "check" in their mind and heart not to emotionally use people. The challenge starts by having you go through your phone and put a star next to anyone of the opposite sex that you feel you have used or potentially could use emotionally, in order to fill a void or a feeling of insecurity—someone you perhaps string along because you enjoy (or need) the affirmation they give you. Maybe it is someone you have a past with and occasionally go back to for emotional or sexual gratification. You know your heart. The stars are there to create a sense of accountability.

When your phone goes off and you see a text message from someone with a star, it is an instant "check" to purify your intentions. Remember, you don't want to use anyone. I know one guy who starred women in his phone and after six months he had deleted them out one by one. He said it was so freeing—no more crutches, no more mixed messages; it forced him to put himself out there, in person, and it changed the way he interacted with other women.

Many women have also used the Cell Phone Challenge to purify their intentions. Before texting someone with a star, evaluate what you are *really* saying—the emotional depth and commitment (or lack of commitment) behind it. Playing games with the heart and the drama and baggage that come from it is damaging to both men and women.

Thank you, men, for taking virtue and Emotional Virtue seriously; I know that you want to protect a woman's heart. I pray that you continue to feel compelled to rise to the level of real love and respect for the women in your lives. Thank you for answering this call.

For the Ladies

All right, women, now you promised not to shoot! When I ask the men "What do you want me to tell the women you struggle with specifically?," they get all shy and sheepish. I prod them. "Look, you begged me to have the conversation that is so hard for you to have. Women need specifics!" Boy, does that open them up. Two hours later, I usually have a notebook full of specifics—what I guess you could call some "secrets" of the male mind. Get your glitter pens ready, ladies; this is very eye opening.

The following are direct quotes from my interviews with men in high school and college:

> Girls have no idea how fast our minds can go from "Oh, I think it's going to rain today," to "Gorgeous girl straight ahead, tight pants, oh my gosh."

> When a girl sits in front of me in class, church, wherever, and is in a strapless dress or shirt, *it's impossible to focus on anything else.* At a wedding, you often only see five bare backs, sitting in the front row!

> When women wear see-through shirts, it is hard not to look for their bra. Even spaghetti straps or thin straps send my mind to bras—neon or black bras under white shirts—gosh, bras.

> Leggings aren't pants. They are just bare legs in a different color. With yoga pants and spandex, it is so hard not to let your eyes go where they shouldn't. And if there is writing on the butt, we try to read it.

> Some shirts and dresses are so low-cut, silky and lacy, it makes me think of the women in lingerie.

Most bikinis have less fabric than bras and under-wear. If I wondered what she looked like under her clothes, I don't have to use my imagination, that's pretty much it.

Okay, ladies, the secrets are out. When men look at you and you are sometimes wondering what they are thinking, unfortunately it may be something like the above. Given the intensity with which many men describe these struggles, I think we can take this as fact.

I also know that some women are completely oblivious that what they wear can have this kind of impact on men. Many women dress to keep up with styles and trends. But sometimes in trying to compete with the fashion of other women, we may be hurting our male friends' battle with purity and their efforts not to objectify or use women's bodies.

On the other hand, some women know exactly what they are doing and "work it" in their favor. They crave the compliments, the "cat calls," and the attention their bodies can arouse. The world definitely encourages women to desire this because they believe sex appeal trumps all—oh, and it sells.

As we've seen, sometimes women will say something like, "It's not my fault if men can't control themselves." But we might reflect upon how we are thinking about this issue. If we're only thinking in minimalistic terms of figuring out at what point we have broken a "rule" or done something wrong, then this objection may have some weight. But if we consider the whole issue—not in a minimalistic way—but in the context of charity and sincere love for the other, the objection falls away. If we view the issue in the context of charity and love, how could we not be concerned with what helps or hurts the other? And the same goes for the men. To say, "It's not my fault if she can't control herself" shows a lack of charity on the man's part.

Modesty of Intentions

Women, we need to reeducate ourselves to see the truth that we are composed of body *and* soul. Don't believe the lie of the world that your self-worth stems only from your body and what your body can "do for you." Your dignity and worth are not equal to your sex appeal; it lies in your profound value and dignity as a human person, a beautiful woman, body and soul *together*. Help men to see you as a whole person, not just body parts.

Men want (and need) to get to know the real you. The way you dress and carry yourself speaks volumes about your confidence and intentions, and so I call it the *Modesty of Intentions*. When you put on an outfit, ask yourself what your intention is; ask yourself in the mirror, "What is my real intention?" If it is to get sexual or emotional attention from men, remember two things: (1) I want you to have confidence in *who* you are and who you are becoming, not in what others think about your body; (2) You know the pitfalls that men can fall into and struggle with; you could be making a choice that may set them back in their efforts to love women for *who* they are.

It is true for both men and women—the way you dress, your body language, the words you speak, the charm, allure, the very aura that surrounds you—all of this speaks to your intentions. Modesty of Intentions calls men and women to be aware and pure in their intentions. The decision to help the opposite sex and not to hurt or set them back in their pursuit of growing in virtue and confidence begins way

before a guy brushes up against a girl or pushes send on a
text—or when a girl finishes getting dressed and walks out
the door. The decision to "help a guy out" or "protect and
respect women" begins with the conversation in your own
head—the conversation in your heart and the "double-
check" of your intentions. The goal is to help each other
in striving for virtue, not to put obstacles in the way.

I love this well-known quote on modesty: "Her clothes
are tight enough to show she is a woman, but loose enough
to show she is a lady." Hear me loud and clear: I am not
saying women are to wear potato sacks with rope belts.
Women don't need to resort to "frumptastic" outfits or
baggie sweatpants and hooded sweatshirts. Keep it classy
—poised, feminine, portraying beauty, and letting your interior confidence shine from within. Show off your personality and style! You *can* do this and still be modest. Is
it harder if you have set a few guidelines for yourself due
to your commitment to your male friends and their future
spouses? Yes, but are they worth it? Is their battle for purity worth it to you? And will they be able to get to know
you at a much deeper level and be able to affirm you as
a whole person in a much deeper way? Yes, because you
will be inviting them to see the whole of who you are, not
just your sex appeal.

A Place to Start

I know women come in all different shapes and sizes and
it is very hard to lay out guidelines, but when I shy away
from particulars, women come to me in private and ask,
"So what *is* modest, really?" They want to know specifics,
parameters—and while mine may be too modest for some
and not modest enough for others, I hope sharing a few
general guidelines to start with may help the cause.

The following are some basic guidelines I set for myself out of love and respect for my husband and all the men out there fighting the good fight. But before I go through them, I want you to know that I am not a wardrobe killjoy. I actually love fashion; my personal style is classy, clean lines, feminine details, stylish accessories, and big jewelry. Putting together outfits that are modest, cute, fun, sophisticated, trendy, and fit my personality has become a challenge I genuinely enjoy. Is it hard at times to find exactly what I need, and do I sacrifice wearing some styles or comfortable outfits for the men in my life? Yes, but the men and their wives or future wives are worth it. I have run this list by many men, and their deep appreciation has been very encouraging to me and other women. So here it goes:

1) I don't own a strapless bra. I have to be able to wear my normal, everyday bra with any outfit, and if my bra is showing, the outfit is out. Dresses (even formal dresses) count here as well. Dresses can be the hardest to find, but they don't get "a pass" just because they can be difficult.

2) Skirts hit the top of my knee when I am standing to ensure that the length is comfortable when I sit. Shorts hit no higher than three inches above my knee when I am standing for the same reason. Men have told me that the issue is not so much the length when we stand, but when we sit. And if skirts are already mid-thigh when we stand, they are more than a distraction when we sit.

3) No spandex. Leggings aren't pants, and yoga pants are legging's little sister, and they are both part of the spandex family.

4) I don't own a bikini. I can't see the difference between someone's bra and underwear and a bikini. Swimsuits

should help you swim and keep you from drowning, not just be a summer fashion statement.

I guess one way to sum up all of these guidelines would be to ask, "How would I want another woman to be dressed in the presence of my boyfriend or husband?"

The Closet Challenge

When we were in college, my friends and I came up with the motto, "If you have to ask, you know the answer!" If you ask yourself or someone else, "Is this too tight? Is this too short? Is this too low cut?" you are already worried about it. Those questions are signs that you are uncomfortable. Clear your conscience and just change or don't buy it. I think most women have probably put on an outfit only to spend the next three hours worrying about how it fits, what it shows, or just being completely uncomfortable. Indeed, there is freedom in what I call the *Closet Challenge*.

Many women across the country have stepped up to take my Closet Challenge. It is definitely that—a major challenge—but just like the Cell Phone Challenge, the women come back to me raving about the new freedom they experience. It goes like this: you invite over your best friend, a family member, or your whole posse— your accountability partners—and you go through your entire closet. You have a full-blown fashion show and try on everything—yes, everything. Here's the kicker: the *accountability partners* decide what is modest and what is not. That's right, you don't get to decide, they do.

If the woman trying on the clothes got to decide, everything would stay—because women can rationalize anything, and we are really good at justifying such things.

Women are often emotionally attached to the clothes in their wardrobe. They can be attached to the memories they've had in them, the compliments they've received in them, and the attention they've gotten over the years. Clothes can become security blankets, and letting them go strikes fear that one may not receive the same compliments or attention in the future.

I understand that fear, but I want you to have freedom. Remember, women, you are more than body parts and sex appeal, and I want your wardrobe to reflect the virtuous, feminine, confident, and committed body and soul that you are. Save your sex appeal for your husband. Your belief in your dignity and worth will shine through as you reveal the beauty of *who* you are.

Friends with Sincere Intentions

When I tell men about women who have taken the Closet Challenge, their reaction is priceless. "Wow, they're really doing that? That's amazing!"

But men, you can take the Closet Challenge as well. Those tight and revealing shirts, pants, and dress suits may need to make a grand exit out of your closet! Women also tell me that it would help if men were more conscious about taking off their shirts at inappropriate times. Both men and women confide in me that they often struggle with the workout wardrobe of the opposite sex. Again, we need to ask ourselves, what is my intention? Is this outfit really furthering my workout, or is it just to get attention? Would I dress the same way if there were no people (or mirrors!) around?

Everyone struggles with different aspects of the Modesty of Intentions, but self-awareness and honesty with yourself and your accountability partners is how you grow. It is virtue in action, and it is instilling the freedom to love.

Thank you for not shooting the messenger. I wanted to share this little piece of what the opposite sex has told me they struggle with. I know it is going to be hard and there will be sacrifices, but you have no idea how much I respect you for considering the Cell Phone Challenge, the Closet Challenge, and all the other challenges you may put into practice as you continue to grow in virtue.

The Modesty of Intentions is very eye-opening. As you grow closer to your posse and also to your friends of the opposite sex, the Modesty of Intentions really comes into play. Your new understanding and awareness of how women can be emotionally charged and how men can be visually stimulated (and vice versa) will serve you well as you learn how to be true *friends*.

That's right, *friends*—not "Which friend am I going to date?" or "My friend with benefits," but true, authentic *friends*. Sharing your life with your posse of women or men and inviting in a posse of the opposite sex will help you to learn how to interact with your friends and how to protect and respect one another.

So you have journeyed with me through ten chapters, and we are knocking on the door of dating. Some of you are probably thinking, "Finally!" Yes, we have finally arrived; but I hope you now have a new view of yourself, your past, your friends, your goals, your priorities, and your future. I also pray that these last ten chapters have given you a fuller view of dating. So let's go for it. Let's build on these chapters and put them into practice. But first, we have one last stop. We have to wade through the fog of what I call the *Gray Area*.

11

THE GRAY AREA : TALKING, TEXTING, AND HANGING OUT

Over the centuries, the idea of finding true love has taken on many forms. In modern times we usually call it dating, a topic that has been the subject of much thought, worry, prayer, and discussion, as well as the cause of many tears.

Dating is a hot topic. I guess you could say it's been a hot topic since the beginning of time—from cavemen, to gladiators, to dukes in the English countryside. It's the first step in answering so many questions like: "Who are you going to choose to spend the rest of your life with? Whose hand are you going to take in marriage? Who is the 'one' you will walk through your life with?"

Dating is complicated—sometimes ridiculously complicated. It seems simple: boy meets girl, they fall in love, and live happily ever after. Don't we all wish it were that easy? As I've mentioned, someone once posed the question to me this way: "Why isn't there some kind of instruction manual for dating? A formula, blueprint, outline, finger-paint drawing—anything! How are we supposed to just know what to do?"

If these thoughts have run through your mind, know that you are not alone. For years I have been trying to figure out this whole "dating thing," especially in the ways it has changed and taken shape in the twenty-first century. I am not going to sugarcoat it: the dating scene is not always a pretty or safe place to be these days; and with social media and texting in the mix—well, let's just say they've been permanent game changers.

There are countless books and loads of advice out there on dating—some great advice and some not-so-great advice. There is no shortage of ideas as to what constitutes dating, including different ways to date and different understandings of various levels of commitment and intimacy—from "We're just talking," "Oh, we're just friends," "We've changed our status," "We just text," to "We're probably getting married someday."

Are We Dating?

I like to ask people, "What do you think dating is? What is the dating scene like around here?" To my surprise, I have been told numerous times that people don't believe "dating" really exists anymore. One guy told me, "You just meet, text, hang out, and then eventually move in together. Dating seems old-fashioned." Some women confided in me that at their university, men and women typically hook up and sleep together a couple of times before the guy deems the girl "worthy" to be taken out on a date—to spend money on her and to actually be seen with her in public.

Wow. Sleep with someone a few times in order to be deemed "worthy" to be officially "dating," if they even want to call it that! I was taken aback; I just shook my head and thought, "Wow. That is so messed up and completely backward. Is this what it has come to? I know we may never go back to the days of carriage rides and front-porch sitting, but is this really what it has to be like?"

As we've said, it is hard to pin down dating because "dating" can mean different things to different people, at different ages and stages in life. Think about the reality of dating in junior high, high school, college, or after college. Oh, and don't forget the "boyfriends and girlfriends" of the elementary school playground!

What does it mean exactly to be "talking" or "texting" or "hanging out?" It is hard to pin down clear answers here because all three of these realities live in what I call the *Gray Area*. I call it the Gray Area because, as implied, it is not black-and-white. It's usually very gray—uncertain and uncommitted: "Are we together or not?" "Are we just friends or something more?" "Do you see us having a future together or are you just using me for right now?"

Texting, Social Media, and the Gray Area

I can recall countless conversations with men and women about the ambiguity, confusion, and frustration of the Gray Area. There appears to be a trend in what they believe to be the main culprits—texting and social media.

As we mentioned in the previous chapter, texting is often a noncommittal way to show interest. One guy told me, "I say so many things in a text that I would never tell a girl in person. It is so much easier to text, especially early on in the relationship, when I can flirt and get to know her without having to risk putting myself out there and fear rejection. If things don't work out, no harm is done. I can just move to the next girl and start texting her."

A high school girl told me, "I don't like eye contact with people, it's awkward, and I avoid it if I can. It is easier to talk or communicate through text or social media." And similarly, this particular conversation with a college guy really got to me. He relayed the following:

> I would never just go up and introduce myself to someone who caught my attention. I always go to social media first, scope it all out, and then make a decision whether or not to get her number. Based on her pictures, posts, feeds, friends, and followers, I can get a pretty good idea of whether or not I want to start "talking" to her.

But as we pointed out, there is often a difference between the "real you" and the "manipulated, perfect social media you." So the person being "scoped" out is likely not the "real me," but the "virtual" version.

I think it is safe to say that texting and social media have changed dating. In fact, I think texting and social media have pretty much changed all relationships. I have watched couples who seem to be on a date eat with one hand and scroll on their phones with the other—rarely looking up or communicating with the person across the table. Parks are filled with parents sitting on benches looking at their phones while their kids play; slumber parties are crowded with junior high girls lounging on couches oblivious to the people around them, just playing on their phones. There is a lot of "communication" going on, but not a lot of face-to-face personal interaction. Because so many people struggle with commitment, availability, and being present to others, it's easy for relationships to remain in the Gray Area.

Now, hear me loud and clear: I'm not saying texting or social media is bad or wrong, or that we should all smash our phones and delete all our social media accounts. The truth is that texting and social media are a way of life, and they are here to stay. Although there are definitely some positives we can take from social media and texting, we have to be aware of how they can negatively affect our relationships as well. The fact is that in the age of social media, we need to make a concerted effort to personally connect with the people around us, especially those closest to us.

Whether it is the attention (or lack thereof) we give to those around us, our friends, our parents, our siblings, coaches, teachers, boss, coworkers, children, whoever is in your life—we need to ask ourselves: Are we truly talking and communicating with them face-to-face? Do they have our full attention? Are we sincerely present and available to them?

What happens when conflict arises? When you encounter a problem, do you know how to work it out and confront someone with honesty and kindness? Fighting or arguing through texts or social media can be downright ugly, and it doesn't always produce the result of figuring it out, resolving the problem, or forgiving and being forgiven.

How does virtue, and especially Emotional Virtue, play out in texting, social media, "talking" and "hanging out"? How do you move through "Hey, nice to meet you," to friends, to dating, to talking about marriage, to getting engaged, and then to walking down the aisle and saying "I do?" And how do you navigate the complicated and difficult journey with virtue—and Emotional Virtue—especially as it pertains to sorting through the Gray Area?

The best place to start might be to look at virtue, and the Simply Irresistible lists, and apply those traits and characteristics to your interactions through social media and texting. The following is one helpful principle to apply to any given situation as it pertains to dating relationships, social media, and texting: as a general rule, *never allow a relationship to go to the next level of intimacy via text or social media; that is, try to keep texting beneath the degree of intimacy to which the relationship has already progressed to that point in time.* This allows the relationship to develop naturally through face-to-face encounters. It also forces both people to put themselves out there in person, by showing interest and nurturing the relationship.

This principle will help us engage the Gray Area constructively. By "Gray Area" here, we mean those times when the relationship enters a "middle zone," either in its beginning or during various transitional stages along the way where the relationship might be moving to a new level, but it is not entirely clear to all parties. Especially at the very beginning of a relationship, social media and texting often make the Gray Area a default mode where interest is often shown in a noncommittal way. Utilizing the principle above (that is, not allowing the relationship to go to the "next step" via social media or texting) helps people to be honest with one another and take the *risk* — the risk of either entering into a relationship or of being rejected. Scary as this may be, what I have seen is that prolonging the Gray Area longer than it needs to be doesn't do anyone any good. Indeed, much of the heartache discussed in this book stems from relationships remaining in this noncommittal Gray Area for far too long.

Calling out the Gray Area and figuring out how to minimize it is crucial for today's relationships, especially in an age of social media and texting. Sincerity and clarity in our communication can prevent a lot of drama and frustration in the end. Although some Gray Area is certainly inevitable at the start of any relationship, we want to be proactive in minimizing it where we can, and not to prolong it unnecessarily.

Moving Beyond the Gray

There are so many questions, and I want this book to be a place of refuge and answers. I want you to use everything I've already presented to help you genuinely communicate with the people in your life.

Building on these truths, I want to give you a "roadmap," a "blueprint," anything that may help navigate dating relationships. I don't have all the answers, and every situation and couple is different, but I've put together a few steps that may help.

But first, it is important to remember that this book is meant to be a *guide*. Its principles are not meant to be a secret potion, where you mix all the ingredients together and calculate every step, believing that with hard and fast precision you will obtain the perfect result or the perfect fairy-tale ending. This book is full of ideas that can help guide you through life and relationships. But in the end, God's ways are not always our ways; and even if we follow the steps of this book perfectly, we still might not find our "happily ever after" in the way we think it should unfold. Still, our Lord is always with us, every step of the way.

And so we start by "beginning with the end in mind." Whether it is trying to put together a bookshelf, completing a science experiment, planning a vacation, winning a state title, landing a dream job, or preparing to be the best wife, husband, mother, or father you can be—if you know what you desire the end goal to look like, then you can start laying out the steps you need to take to get there. The same is true for relationships. In the last chapter, we will lay out the steps we need to take to reach our goal. With a little more detail than a finger-paint drawing, we will map out what I call the *Natural Progression of a Relationship*.

THE NATURAL PROGRESSION
OF A RELATIONSHIP

Andy and I were standing around with a group of college men and women as we chatted about the realities of dating and finding a spouse, and finally one girl came out and said, "We've decided that dating is just plain scary. We've come to the realization that with every person you date, the relationship will end in one of two ways—you either get married or you break up, and *that* is terrifying." Whoa, I thought, I had never thought about it quite like that before, but she was right. When you start dating someone, the destination of the journey is either "I do's" on the altar, or the potential heartache of a breakup.

That is a harsh and startling reality, but it is also true. I don't think many people stop to think about it that way; but when you do, it changes the way you look at the dating scene, and I think it is a good place to start the conversation about contemporary relationships.

As we discussed in the previous chapter, it is hard to nail down a definition of dating because of the many different forms it can take before the "I do's" of marriage. Many people don't believe in marriage anymore, or don't want to get married because of the fears, wounds, and pain they have experienced from marriages that have fallen apart.

It's true: if divorce hasn't affected us directly, we surely know others who have been wounded by it, or perhaps have felt the pain of a marriage that stayed together but was altogether unhappy.

I guess that is just another reason why I wanted to write this book and especially this chapter on relationships. There has to be a better way. There has to be an alternative to the sadness, brokenness, and pain. While I don't have all the answers—and even if I did, relationships still wouldn't be easy—I desire nothing more than happiness, joy, excitement, and peace in your relationships, and especially for your marriage someday.

Whatever has happened in the past is now in the past; and although it has affected you, it doesn't need to define you moving forward. You have a new awareness and a plan that gives you the power to transform both yourself and the way you navigate relationships.

As you read this, you may find yourself single, in a serious relationship, in a brand-new relationship, or coming out of a horrible breakup. Whether you have had ten different relationships, two, twenty, or zero, I want you to take a look at what I call the *Natural Progression of a Relationship* and see how it applies to you—in your stage of life, or at your stage in a relationship right now—as a plan that aims always to begin with the end in mind.

Nowadays, we don't have many places to turn to in order to learn how to date or, simply how to pursue someone in a relationship. Relationships seem to "just happen" and when things are "just happening," the Gray Area seems to get grayer and grayer and grayer.

Meet, date, and move in together is one plan, and a very popular one in today's culture; or hook up, have sex, (maybe) date, and move in together. But if dating relationships end in marriage or a breakup, I think we may need to add a few more steps in our plan—especially since we want to find an alternative to the drama, heartache, and pain.

So here we go, the Natural Progression of a Relationship:

1. Acquaintances

2. True Friends

3. Defining the Relationship—Having a DTR

4. Dating

5. Courting

6. Engagement

7. Marriage

Okay, you may be thinking, "What is a DTR? What is courting? And True Friends might be the cheesiest thing I have ever heard of." But before you write me off, let's walk through each step and I will explain why I think each of them (and their particular order) is so important. As we go along, I will also introduce my *Formula for Moving Forward* in relationships: *God, virtue, time, trust, and honesty.* As you move through every step in the Natural Progression of a Relationship, you can evaluate whether or not to move forward based on this formula.

1. Acquaintances

You meet someone. You may have just met this person, or you may have known him or her your whole life. You may already be tempted to let mental stalking run wild in your mind, but let's pull back on the reins a bit and hold this in check. I first want you to desire to be their friend. This person may start and end as just a friend or something more; but friendship first is a *win-win* because even if you don't get married, you still have a good friend. God, virtue, time, trust, and honesty: Is this someone who is running or wants to run with you toward our Lord? Is he or she striving for virtue? Has time allowed for you to trust this person, and do you feel like you can be honest with them? If so, great, strengthen that friendship.

2. *True Friends*

Believe it or not, this is probably one of the most important steps. By True Friends here, I mean both (a) the importance of building a relationship upon a friendship first and (b) the importance of one's larger posse and family as the setting in which a relationship is best able to begin and develop.

As I laid out in Chapter 9 (Finding Your Posse), the importance of finding friends who make you better and help you grow is one of the most important things you can take away from this book. After you have that set in place and are investing in those relationships, find a posse of the opposite sex, and *be friends!* Go places together, have fun together, get creative, build each other up, help one another out, support each other at sporting events and performances, go have ice cream, go bowling, go to the movies, do service projects together, study together, go to dances together—*share life together.* Be creative, make memories, and get to know one another better!

Now notice that I didn't say, "Spend all your time trying to figure out which member of the opposite sex you are going to date?" No, you are building up true, authentic, lasting, lifelong friendships. It's important that you learn how to be *friends* with members of the opposite sex before you try to date any of them.

The reason why establishing solid friendships is so important is because anyone can go out with you on a Friday night at 7 p.m.—for a fabulous evening with dinner, a movie, dancing, a walk under the stars, and then back home at midnight—and be the perfect date (and person) for exactly five hours. You only get to know the person as the perfect date—telling you exactly what you want to hear, doing whatever you want to do. But know that at the stroke of midnight, he or she can easily go back to being whoever he or she was at 6:59 p.m.

Because of the Gray Area, people can also be the "perfect" date (and person) via text and social media without having to ever leave their houses—telling you exactly what you want to hear, checking up on you throughout your day, and telling you how amazing you are before you drift off to sleep. The scary thing is that you don't know how many other people are getting these exact same texts. You may not be the only one.

Becoming True Friends is crucial for two main reasons. First, it is your "check." How does this guy or girl act around your friends? How does she act around her own friends and family? How does that guy treat other women, especially women he's *not* interested in? How does this girl act around the guys? Are her actions consistent? Is this guy or girl striving for virtue in the way they treat other people, not just you? What is most important to them? Do they share your beliefs, morals, and convictions? Are they striving to be emotionally virtuous, and are they aware of mixed signals, confusing flirtation, and the Gray Area?

Many men and women share stories with me about a close friend who started dating someone he or she didn't really know and now they are worried about their friend, because their friend has seemingly dropped them for this significant other, often no longer returning texts or calls. Moving from Acquaintances to Dating without True Friends misses this "check." If your closest, most beloved, and trusted friends, or your family are worried or have reservations about the person you are dating, that is a red flag. You need to hear them out. You may not agree with their evaluation of the person or the situation, but you should at least listen to what they have to say and be open to an honest conversation. They love and care for you; they want to protect you and help you grow in faith and virtue. And if the person you are dating, or are thinking about dating, doesn't pass the "check" by your friends who love you, then your friends have the obligation in charity to look out for you; you would do the same for them.

The second reason this step of becoming True Friends is so crucial is that it helps to minimize the Gray Area. Instead of getting to know someone *primarily* through text or social media, you are getting to know someone primarily through face-to-face communication. The time you used to spend scrolling and even over-romancing is spent truly getting to know him—asking questions, telling stories, interacting with him around the people he cares for, and actually *doing* things with those friends, instead of just watching your interactions play out on a screen.

Notice I said "primarily" because I know that texting and social media will still play a role in your life and relationships, but be aware and maybe even a little cautious of how much of a role it plays in your interactions with the opposite sex, especially at the beginning stages of a potential relationship. If we are going to stay off the Emoticoaster and try to minimize the Gray Area, we have to practice virtue and especially Emotional Virtue. Be very careful about sending mixed messages or emotionally charged texts or posts. Remember, we made the commitment not to use others or to be used, emotionally or physically; and these are your *friends,* your greatest friends of the opposite sex. We need to respect them and protect them.

Along with respecting and protecting your friends, be very aware of what you choose to do when you all spend time together. If every choice you make is taking you one step closer or further away from who you want to be, the same goes for the group as a whole.

Based on the foundations of this whole book, it's important to reevaluate what you enjoy doing for fun. I have to be honest with you—*drunkenness equals drama.* Period. Getting drunk or getting high at a party or a club leads to drama usually in the form of a chick fight (usually over a guy), a fight between two men (usually over a girl), or a fight between a guy and a girl (usually between a boyfriend and girlfriend over some other guy or girl). If the fight doesn't happen that day or night when everyone is drunk, it will play out in the following days or weeks, and will sometimes involve people who were not even there. Drunkenness equals drama, and I am pretty sure that life can be dramatic enough the way it is. I don't think we need to add fuel to the fire.

I know that finding a posse, investing in them, growing with them, and then finding a posse of the opposite sex and befriending them and growing in virtue can be a tall order. It will be hard work at times, and you will definitely have to be creative about where you go and what you do together. Use everything you are learning in this book to put yourself (and your posse) in places and situations where you don't have to take steps backward from who you want to be. Trust me, the effort is worth it; some of my greatest memories are from the times when my posse of best girl friends and guy friends were together. To this day, I am still close to friends from that posse, and I am so grateful for them and the time we invested in each other. I wouldn't be the person I am today without them.

So you've met; you're friends and have been getting to know each other in your posse—learning how to interact with the opposite sex, respecting, protecting, and growing in virtue, all the while having a ridiculously good time and making memories. But over time, you start to notice that one member of the opposite sex keeps standing out in the crowd. You are friends; he or she passes the "check" with your friends (probably because he or she is already good friends with them as well), and you are ready to apply the Formula for Moving Forward: God, virtue, time, trust, and honesty. Is this someone who is running with you toward our Lord? Is he striving for virtue? Has time allowed for you to trust him, and do you feel like you can be honest with him? Great! I'm glad you are friends, and it seems like there might be something more going on. It's time for a DTR.

3. Defining the Relationship—Having a DTR

Moving from True Friends to Dating is notorious for being confusing, frustrating, complicated, puzzling, muddy, or, as we've said, just gray. That's right, the Gray Area will try to creep into the Natural Progression of a Relationship, but you can minimize it—with a DTR.

You have to define the relationship. "I think he likes me." "I think there is something more going on." "I think she treats me differently than the other guys." "I think I like him as more than a friend." "I think I like her as more than a friend." As these thoughts pop into your mind, and as you reflect and pray about whether or not you want to move forward in a relationship with this person, it is important to ask yourself, "What are my intentions?" Make sure you are not using, manipulating, or trying to fill insecurities or holes. What is your intention? If you feel like God is calling you to move forward and see if there is more to this relationship than just friendship, then state your intentions and pursue a relationship. But please, don't get to this point, and instead of making known how you feel, spend the next six months flirting, just "talking, texting, and hanging out" together in the Gray Area.

But as we know, it is difficult to state your intentions for many reasons. For one, it is easier and more comfortable to cozy up in the Gray Area and not commit to someone, or to semi-commit to a handful of people. Stating your intentions requires putting yourself out there, being honest and courageous, and facing the possibility of rejection. I know that is hard, but it is so important if we are going to minimize the Gray Area and allow authentic friendships to grow into solid dating relationships.

Stating your intentions is also difficult because of the fact that by doing so you are potentially entering into a commitment that could either lead to dating, courting, and marriage, or it could lead to a breakup and possible heartache—or, of course, instant rejection. I do not want you to fear stating your intentions or entering into a dating relationship with someone. But I also don't think you should date just "for fun," or to just "casually date around."

You shouldn't date someone who isn't the type of person you would like to marry one day. It just doesn't make sense to enter into that relationship, even if it is just dipping your pinkie toe in, if he or she isn't the type of person you could see yourself marrying. Before entering any relationship, you should be able to say "yes" to this question: does this person exhibit the faith, character, and virtue I hope to find in my future spouse and the mother/father of my children someday? Of course, this particular person may well not be "the one." But the person you choose to date should possess a similar virtuous and faithful character to what you hope to find in "the one." If you did "fall in love" while casually dating around but you knew he or she wasn't right for you over the long haul, you would only be setting yourselves up for heartache, and I don't want that for either of you.

Instead of dating for fun or casually dating around, if you want to get to know someone, invite him out with you and your friends. Get to know him as a friend. It is important to let your family and your friends get to know him; start down the path of the Natural Progression of a Relationship. As we've said, your family and this group of friends (male and female) will be a "buffer" and a check—and certainly a big help in growing in Emotional Virtue. It is hard to let a "flirtfest" run wild with all your male and female friends around without anyone noticing that something more might be going on. But it can easily go unnoticed if it takes place only in texts and on social media, or in an exclusive dating relationship that avoids contact with your closest friends and family. You need your accountability partners who will (kindly and privately) help you sort out your intentions and actions, so that friendship can truly come first.

A special word for the men: as hard as it may be, you truly are the leaders in this "stating your intentions" step. I know it is difficult to know what to do and how to "properly pursue a woman," and the world is definitely not doing you any favors; but just as the Simply Irresistible Virtuous

Man list reads "leader, provider, initiator, protector," a man should lead with virtue, provide clarity, initiate conversation, and protect each woman. Every woman you meet is someone's daughter, sister, or friend, and those fathers, brothers, and friends are relying on you to protect her in the same way they would.

No playing games with the heart, no emotional manipulation—just honesty, integrity, and clarity. This could be your future wife you are pursuing; and if it is not your future wife, it could be your best friend's future wife. Wow, let's all just sit with that for a minute! You could date, or maybe are dating, your best friend's future wife. If that doesn't change the way we view dating or how we should navigate the Natural Progression of a Relationship, I don't know what will! If she is called to marriage, this woman is someone's future wife, so try to lead with virtue, provide clarity, initiate conversation, protect her purity, and state your intentions.

The goal (and this goes for both men and women) should be the following: imagine meeting the spouse of someone you dated in the past and having him or her be able to look you in the eye and honestly say, "Thank you. My husband/wife is a better person because of the time he/she spent with you." This is a tall order, but what makes it possible is putting what is best for the other person always first and foremost, being responsible for the other person for whatever amount of time you spend with him or her.

Now women, in order for the men to have confidence and take on this endeavor, it's important to remember three things:

1. Men are not mind readers.

2. Men have most likely not been taught how to do this and there is no manual.

3. When a man states his intentions, he is asking to get to know you better and to see if you are called to date and take a serious step forward in your relationship; however, this is *not* a marriage proposal.

Men tell me how intimidating it is to get the guts to state their intentions (after all, she could say no). They spend weeks mustering up the courage and making sure it is the right thing to do, only to have a girl respond to his coffee or dinner invitation with, "Sure, and I'd like to have a house in the country with a white picket fence, five kids, and you can be a doctor or a lawyer, whichever you'd like!"

It is the Natural *Progression* of a Relationship. Progression means development, advancement, growth, happening *naturally* over time. God, virtue, time, trust, and honesty build what will last—that is the Formula for Moving Forward. If you like someone, find ways to drop hints, perhaps even saying something like, "I appreciate your friendship; I would like to get to know you better." If the other person shares your affection, then he or she will eventually pick up your hints. Now if you find yourself dropping hint after hint with no response, then it may be the case that the other person does not share the same interest and eventually we have to accept that for what it is and move on. Naturally, what usually happens is *friends* will find themselves out with a big group and as everyone is starting to leave, they notice that they are still talking, something starts to click, and cues are given. When you start to notice something or think something is up, start to think on it, pray about it, and be honest. Then when the time is right, men, state your intentions; and the women (at least the ones who have read this book) will know that it is not a marriage proposal. So have confidence and go for it!

I'm sure you are thinking, "Oh, Sarah, and what was that you said about rejection?" Good question. I didn't forget. Yes, rejection or liking someone who doesn't reciprocate the same level of attraction does happen, and it is hard; again, no sugarcoating here. But here's the deal: Men, if you take the Natural Progression to heart and start off as acquaintances and then authentic friends, and state your intentions to get to know one of your female friends better and pursue dating her, and she says, right then and there, "I value your friendship, but I truly see us as just friends," it is going to sting a bit, yes, but now you know. There is no six-month flirtfest in the Gray Area; there are no "I wonder ifs." You have your answer and you can move on. You know that she is a good friend, but you're not called or meant to date, not right now, maybe not ever. If she changes her mind, she will find a way to let you know. But don't just sit around and wait on it. Live your life, grow in friendship and virtue with other friends, and be ready to state your intentions if you feel called to move forward with another woman down the road.

Ladies, the same principles apply. Let's say you like a guy friend. You have dropped every hint in the book, and even said, "Thanks for your friendship. I would love to get to know you better," and he responds, "I value your friendship, but I truly see us as just friends." Yes, it is going to sting, but thank God for clarity. See him as the friend that he is, put Emotional Virtue on high alert, and don't wait around. You may miss the guy who wants to pursue a relationship with you if you are obsessed with a guy who just wants to be your friend.

A final word on DTRs: while there is inevitably a bit of "gray" in the time leading up to the DTR and even immediately following, one principle that can minimize the difficulty and confusion is this: *make sure you are pursuing a*

DTR with only one person at a time. This will better signal interest and commitment to the person you are interested in, also minimizing the Gray Area and avoiding mixed messages. If you keep the step toward a potential DTR and Dating to one person at a time, it will remove a lot of confusion and prevent possible heartache and frustration.

Lastly, there may need to be a second DTR of sorts. The first one would be the initial showing of interest ("I appreciate your friendship and I would like to get to know you better"), which opened the door to the *possibility* of dating. Often, a second DTR is needed later, when the two become an actual couple and an exclusive commitment is made. The time between the first DTR and the second is a time of discernment. Although there is no magic formula, it shouldn't be too long. When this period is prolonged, it simply turns into an ongoing Gray Area, which can result in a lot of hurt and confusion. Bravely taking the risk of putting oneself out there at both of these points is crucial; honesty and courage here will save much heartache in the end.

I know all this is easier said than done, but we have no time for prolonging the Gray Area any longer than it has to be. We need honesty, clarity, and true, authentic friendship. But let's say that a guy friend states his intentions to his female friend and she says, "Yes, I would really like to get to know you better, too. I would love to go to dinner with you. Thank you." Well, the intentions have been stated on both sides and we've taken the time to run it through the Formula for Moving Forward—God, virtue, time, trust, and honesty: Is this someone who is running toward our Lord and would make a great running partner? Is she striving for virtue? Has time allowed for you to trust her and do you feel like you can be honest with her? If not, be honest with her; talk with her about how you are feeling, your hesitations or worries. Being honest upfront will save you heartache later on. But, if you have looked at this new relationship through the lens of God, virtue, time, trust, and honesty and feel called to proceed, let's make it official and move to dating.

4. Dating

Well, we're here. The phrase "we're officially dating" has been spoken. One of my goals with laying out every step of the Natural Progression of a Relationship is to break down each one of them, and define them so that they don't get blurred or muddied. As I have said, I am a fan of beginning with the end in mind, and also a big fan of keeping things as clear as possible.

I like to highlight the differences between True Friends, Dating, and Courting because when both people are not on the same page or moving at similar paces, things can get awfully messy.

I want to very clearly and carefully define the role of dating in contrast to courting. Dating occurs after moving from Acquaintances to friends, spending time in the posse and getting to know someone as a True Friend, and allowing all the natural "checks" to take place in your own heart and within your trusted posse. Through dating, your main goal is to continue to get to know someone and deepen the solid friendship that has already begun. Getting to know someone one-on-one and investing in this relationship is exciting, but we need to recognize and remember a few important things: (1) Saying yes to a dating relationship is not saying yes to a marriage proposal, or receiving a yes to a marriage proposal. (2) Your relationship as a dating couple should not look *drastically* different than when you were True Friends. Please, do not drop your other friends and family. Make every effort to balance your time between your friends and family and your new significant other. Just because you are officially dating doesn't mean that you stop investing in your posse, or that the two of you stop spending time with your big posse and families. Those relationships do not move to the back burner; in fact, it is more important than ever to have those friendships thriving in your life, because your friends and family will help you navigate the next steps. (3) Remember that this is either going to end in marriage or a breakup.

I do not want you to be scared to enter into a dating relationship, but it must be taken seriously. Always return to the Formula for Moving Forward—God, virtue, time, trust, and honesty. Is this someone who is holding you accountable in your pursuit of virtue and running with you toward our Lord? Has time allowed for you to trust his words and his actions? Do you feel like you can be honest with him? I want you to pursue this dating relationship with this question in mind: "Can I see myself possibly *moving toward* marriage with this person in the future?"

Now, if at any point you evaluate the relationship honestly and feel as though you are hesitant to move forward for some reason, it is best to lead with virtue and communicate with the person you are dating face-to-face (not primarily through texting and social media). Here is where, as wonderful as the heart is, it cannot lead; the head needs to be in the driver's seat. Discernment needs to be based on the truth and reality of the other person and of the relationship, not just the accompanying emotions and feelings. Be honest with the person you are dating, and most of all, be honest with yourself.

Just because you are in a dating relationship doesn't mean the temptation to use someone—to fill insecurities, or to make you feel whole, or to gratify you in some way emotionally or physically—goes away or doesn't apply. Please don't stay in dating relationships out of fear—fear that you will never find someone else, fear that this is the only person who will ever love you, fear that you will lose the feeling of love, or fear that you could never find someone "better."

No relationship can be free and grow if it is chained down by fear. That is why this whole book is a guide on how to date. As men and women of faith and virtue, we need to strive and train and prepare in order to be able to enter into a dating relationship and be *free* to love, discern, grow, serve, and clearly evaluate whether or not you are supposed to move forward with this person toward marriage. Never settle just because you think you can't do "better." If you are not chained down by fear, or by the addiction of love as only a feeling, then you will be able to see clearly when a dating relationship just isn't quite right. You will be free to walk away. It may be hard, but you will not be devastated because you are not dependent upon love as a feeling. You are striving to be confident, virtuous, whole, joyful, and free—someone who will go to our Lord and lay down this relationship at His feet, letting Him love you and guide you.

If a dating relationship is being evaluated through the Formula for Moving Forward, and all signs point to moving forward, I might ask you, "Do you feel called to enter a courting relationship with this person?" That's right, courting. It is a foreign word to many of us, but one of the most important things we can do to succeed in dating relationships is to distinguish Dating from Courting. The word courting seems to have been firmly locked away in a vault along with virtue, modesty, and Jane Austen, but I think we should pull them all back out and insert them back into our twenty-first-century vocabulary.

5. Courting

Gentlemen, if you have ever listened to women talk about Jane Austen novels, you have probably heard them swooning over the long-ago days of a "suitor" coming to the house —all dapper and clean-shaven, with a bouquet of fresh-picked wildflowers, knocking on the front door to ask the father for the honor of the lady's hand to accompany him on an evening stroll. Insert long female sigh.

The only familiarity I had with the word courting was definitely this image. Courting is a word that seems to be completely lost to our generation; and while, yes, things have changed and the Natural Progression of a Relationship doesn't pretend to exist in the world of a nineteenth-century romantic fiction, I think bringing Courting back into our discussion could be helpful.

Some might say, "Sarah, aren't dating and courting the same thing?" I have definitely heard this before, and although there may be overlap, it is important to make a distinction, precisely for the sake of Emotional Virtue. Men get nervous about pursuing a woman because it is easy for a woman to think that by a man stating his intentions about wanting to pursue a dating relationship, she might see it as a marriage proposal and actually go out and buy the dress she secretly has picked out. Or, a man states his intentions and the woman says she would like to get to know him better in a dating relationship, and in his head (or at an actual jewelry shop) he starts picking out rings.

Dating is pursuing a relationship in order to get to know someone better, with the hope of continuing through the Formula for Moving Forward. Courting is taking a serious step toward marriage and discerning the question: "Lord, is this the person you have called me to marry and share my life with? Is this the person you desire me to serve You with—running side by side, raising a family together, growing in faith and virtue for a lifetime?"

How beautiful are those questions? This is real life, and courting is a big step with big questions. Do you see the difference between Dating—"I want to get to know you better and see if I'm called to pursue a deeper commitment" —versus Courting—"Am I called to marry this person? Is this the person God has called me to serve Him with?"

Although there is no magic threshold through which a couple passes when they go from Dating to Courting, it's safe to say that when the topic of marriage begins to be discussed in any kind of serious fashion (and is also realistically in sight), the couple has probably moved into the Courting phase (regardless of whether or not they call it that).

Courting is one step away from Engagement. And in courting, the Formula for Moving Forward becomes an even more intense and deeper look into the relationship: God, virtue, time, trust, and honesty. As you are evaluating whether or not to move forward, I want to offer a few questions to help apply the Formula for Moving Forward. These questions are particularly appropriate for this juncture, in the movement from Dating to Courting.

As you get further along in the Natural Progression of a Relationship and choosing a spouse, I think it is safe to say that setting your priorities and knowing not only what you want and need in a spouse, but *what God wants and needs for you in a spouse* is something not to be taken lightly. So here are a few questions to ask yourself as you prepare to take the next step toward marriage:

1) God: Where does his faith rank in his life? Does he pursue a relationship with God? Do you let God into your relationship and allow Him to guide you, love you, and support you?

2) Virtue: Is she actively striving for virtue? What does she think of the Simply Irresistible lists? Do you see her striving and trying to overcome struggles and vice in her life and to pursue virtue? Do you help and encourage each other to grow in virtue?

3) Time: Have you let time naturally guide your relationship and not rushed things? Do you feel like you have had enough time to evaluate this relationship for the next step? Have you both been consistent and persistent in showing your love through sacrifice and in difficult times, not just in the good or easy times?

4) Trust: Has time allowed for you to trust him and do you feel like you are your true self with him? Do you trust him to pursue a selfless love, and not a selfish love, when it comes to the emotional and physical aspects of your relationship? Do you trust him to protect you, not to put you in compromising situations, and not to use you? Have you earned his trust? Are you looking out for the good of one another?

5) Honesty: Can you be completely honest with this person and with yourself? Do you communicate in a way that is clear? Do you feel understood, and do you strive to understand? Are you "heard" and do you listen well? Can

you be yourself around her and can you freely strive for virtue? Do you find an honest running mate beside you?

These are the types of questions that should guide the Natural Progression of a Relationship and your decision to move forward through each step, but especially as you discern whether the relationship should take a more serious turn.

Whether you are reading this as a couple in a courting relationship, a single person who is considering defining the relationship with someone soon, or a married person who has been married for thirty-plus years, I bet many of you are saying, "Wow, those questions hit home as to what is *truly* important."

This Formula for Moving Forward is an amazing conversation waiting to happen. I didn't say it was going to be an easy or comfortable conversation, and it probably won't be one conversation but hundreds of conversations over the course of your relationship. I know many of you may find it very difficult to share these questions with your significant other, but using this list as a guide and "check" for your relationship could be the link that holds your marriage together in the future—and not only the link that holds it together, but the bond that makes it stronger.

It will certainly bring clarity on which direction your relationship should take and where you need to grow, and clarity will bring peace and joy in the end—whether that means knowing when to move forward, or when to walk away. Even when a relationship has ended, the Formula for Moving Forward comes into play: God (turn to Him), virtue (let it guide your thoughts, words, and actions); time (it will take time, but wounds do heal); trust (trust God, yourself, and your True Friends and family to see you through this difficult time); and honesty (be honest with God, yourself, and others).

That is one of the questions I get asked the most, "Sarah how do I get through this breakup?" This whole book in many ways is my answer to that question. Run to the Lord, and apply the Formula for Moving Forward to your situation; with time, your pain will heal; and try your best to focus on what matters most (things like—Real Life's Big Three, faith, virtue, family, and friends). Don't go into stall mode: the more you get moving toward the real goal of life—growing in faith and virtue—the more your heart will begin to heal. But still, it will take time.

6. *Engagement*

I think almost every little girl has dreamt about the day she would be proposed to, and many little girls have had fun acting out the proposal at recess on the playground. Many young women get misty-eyed as they watch videos of amazing proposals online, and countless pinboards are filled with ideas for rings, gowns, invitations, and even possible places where they would like to be proposed to.

I know men also spend hours, maybe even days, thinking up and planning the "perfect" proposal. A lot of time and energy is spent on how the marriage proposal is going to happen, but in the Natural Progression of a Relationship, engagement is more than just the proposal.

Engagement is the final step before the altar and the vows. Engagement is the time right before the most important decision of your life—the vows you declare on your wedding day. Engagement is an amazing time of joy, anticipation, planning, and excitement. But it is not just preparation for the wedding day; it is also a time of deep discernment—a time for prayer and preparation for a life-long marriage.

Engagement is a step that gets overlooked all too often. You may be thinking: "Overlooked! Someone gets engaged and then everyone springs into action! There are venues to be booked and caterers to hire, flowers to be chosen, the music, the honeymoon, dresses, tuxes, and fifteen different cakes to be tested! Overlooked? It's all about being engaged!"

But the importance of the step of engagement is often overlooked by the couple themselves. Yes, there are a ton of things to do, and yes, there are entire Web sites dedicated to the twenty-five page checklists for getting the wedding just perfect. But my worry is that in the hustle and bustle of planning for the wedding day, couples forget to plan and prepare for their marriage. One lasts roughly twelve hours, the other a lifetime.

I once asked a large group of college women, "Do engagements get called off?" There was a sad, slow nodding of four hundred heads. Then I asked, "Should more engagements probably be called off than actually are?" There was an even sadder, and slower, nodding of four hundred heads. This wasn't an attack on any one couple; I was just trying to make the point that until you are on the altar—ready to make solemn vows in front of God, your family, friends, and to each other—it is still a time of preparation and discernment. At this point, one needs to look at the Formula for Moving Forward *more*, not less. There isn't a more important time to walk through that list as a couple and make sure—very sure—that you are on the same page and ready to move forward as husband and wife.

Many people get engaged and think, "Yep, this is it, we can move in together, sleep together, join our bank accounts, get a dog, plan our wedding—we're getting married!" Instead of planning and preparing for the single most important decision of their life, people "jump the gun" and easily become distracted by the elated emotions of being engaged. So caught up in "getting married," many of the red flags—moments of anxiety and doubt, difficult and much-needed conversations—are pushed down and pushed away for the sake of the excitement and the 982 things that need to be done before the big day.

When God knocks on the door of the heart, when the friend voices concern, or when that nagging voice from within tries for the umpteenth time to get your attention, the answer too often is a firm: "Go away, I'm too far into this, I've given this person everything, I'm happy, we're getting married, we have the tux and the dress, five hundred invitations are in the mail, and I am not backing out now. I don't care what you say, even if I know this doesn't seem right, even if I know this probably won't last, I'm not starting over."

One doesn't need to have an engagement ring picked out or wedding invitations in the mail to suffer from feeling trapped in a relationship. Many men and women get into serious relationships only to find that reading through things like the Formula for Moving Forward stir up an immense amount of pain, uncertainty, and even fear. At any point of the Natural Progression of a Relationship, if you feel trapped or worried about an aspect of your relationship, be honest and bring it to light. Here, especially, it can be easy for couples to use sex as a type of Band-Aid to heal or cover up wounds; but sex is often a blinding (and binding) force that doesn't clarify or bring things to light, but actually clouds things by making them seem better than they are. You have to communicate honestly, respect-fully, and lovingly with your significant other. Suppressing, burying, or covering up fears or concerns will only hurt your relationship and stunt its growth and progression. I know that it may be hard to hear, but my husband Andy and I often say this to young couples seeking advice: "The struggles you have before marriage do not go away on your wedding day. Not only do they not disappear, they are magnified in marriage."

Asking hard questions and truly getting on the same page is a key component of Engagement. I am married and I remember planning our wedding; I know the months leading up to a wedding are an extremely busy and stress-ful time; but it is important to take the time to prepare and grow closer through communication, faith, and virtue, as you let the Formula for Moving Forward guide those im-portant conversations. After all, this is the most important decision and day of your life. The more thoughtful and prayerful the preparation, the less likely either person will find regret and heartache in the end.

Well, say you've met, developed a true friendship with a rock-solid foundation, stated your intentions, got to know one another better through dating, applied the Formula for Moving Forward every step of the way, prayed and asked the hard questions in courting, extended or accepted a beautiful engagement ring, and put in all the hard work of navigating the entire Natural Progression of a Relationship. Wow, you've done it! I know it has not been easy and there may have been a few bumps along the way, but I know it has all been so worth it! And I am proud of you—"We're going to the chapel, and we're gonna get married!"

7. *Marriage*

I want you to go back and look at the Simply Irresistible Virtuous Woman and the Simply Irresistible Virtuous Man lists. Can you imagine this couple—each *striving* for virtue, Christ at the center of their lives, always looking out for what is best for the other person—coming together and dating? All the more, can you imagine this couple standing before the altar on their wedding day?

Every single day before they stood before the altar was a day of *preparation*. That couple knew that every decision they made along the way, big or small, was taking them closer or further away from the man or woman they desired to be on their wedding day and throughout their marriage. They knew that what they let into their hearts and minds was *forming* them, molding and shaping their desires, passions, and emotions, and influencing who they were becoming.

They wanted to be strong for each other and ready for whatever life threw at them—ready for the sacrifices, suffering, and hard times that would come along in life. That couple understood that self-awareness and self-mastery went hand in hand—they knew who they wanted to be; they strove to keep their passions and emotions ordered and harnessed, and they tried to master the selfishness that can surface by transforming themselves into the kind of people who were able and capable of choosing the true, the good, and the beautiful.

True love is not a needy love; true love is gift love. True love and virtue allow one to rise up and love another person as if they were another self—to seek the good of the other as if it were your own; not simply to love for what you get in return, or for some gratification you receive in return, but for the other's own sake. This is married love—it is the gift of your very self.

You give your whole self to your spouse in marriage: emotionally, spiritually, and physically. The Natural Progression of a Relationship progresses over time, revealing a little more about you at each step, and it is all leading to the summit, to the peak, to the culmination of that long journey you have spent years preparing for—the day that you are truly unveiled for your beloved to behold.

I've written this book because I don't want you to be held captive by the World's Idea of Perfect, the Emoticoaster, and the Cycle of Use; I want you to seize every moment of your life and grow in virtue and closeness with our Lord. When I look at the Simply Irresistible lists, I get excited; I get excited for that couple coming together, and I get excited for *you!* These are the friendships and relationships I want you to encounter; and this is the mind-blowing *marriage* I want for you, the family I want for you, and the freedom to be the husband and father or the wife and mother that you truly long to be.

But as we have said, in order to make this happen, we need preparation. Here is where chastity comes in. Sometimes when people hear the word chastity, they immediately think of it in a negative sense. "Yeah, yeah, Sarah, don't have sex till you're married . . . We know, we know, don't do this, don't do that, don't, don't, don't." I think some people see chastity as the culprit for taking away their "fun." The word chastity can get many eyes to roll and many minds to completely tune out—"Here we go again, rules, rules, rules."

When you say "no" to something, you are saying "yes" to something else. When you choose *against* something, you are choosing *for* something else. By saying no to sex and sleeping with someone before marriage, you are saying yes to "I love you for your own sake" and "I don't want to use you." By saying no to sexual activity before marriage, you are saying yes to giving all of yourself to your future spouse; by saying no to sex, you are saying yes to freeing yourself to love someone more than you love yourself, putting his or her good above your own emotional and physical desires. By saying no to sex, you are not only protecting the purity of your future spouse, you are also strengthening his or her relationship with God. And if true love wills the good of the other, true love wills and fosters the greatest of all goods, namely, his or her relationship with God.

Chastity is not just a no, but a yes to striving to become the woman of your dreams or the man you're called to be. Chastity is a yes to the man or the woman who will be waiting for you at the altar, even though you may not be able to see them right now; they do exist, and your yes to loving them *now* is the greatest, most loving, selfless, virtuous gift you could ever give them. Your yes to chastity is preparing you to be *free* to give your whole self to them— emotionally, spiritually, and physically—on your wedding day and forever.

Chastity is a virtue, and the "rules" to play by in virtue or in morality are there so that we don't destroy ourselves or anyone else; even more, they are there to lead us to *true happiness.* Someone once explained it to me this way: imagine your relationship is like a grand and beautiful house, and in that house there is a fireplace—massive, oak, ornate, and stunning. You put the firewood in the fireplace, light the match, and enjoy the warmth and romantic ambiance. The fireplace is marriage—where sex is not only safe and secure but is an incredible gift from God. The fire is our sexual hunger and intimacy; and if it's not used in its right time and setting, it will actually bring great harm. So, imagine that beautiful house again with no fireplace in it: if you lit a fire in the middle of your living room, you would burn your whole house to the ground.

I remember sharing this with a group of college women and one girl looked at me completely dumbfounded and said, "So you're saying that I can't have sex with anyone until my wedding night? No one, not even my fiancé, the man I *know* I'm going to marry, I can't even sleep with him until my wedding night?" Her eyes widened with shock as she continued, "Sex is great. I love having sex. I don't think I could live without it."

I asked her, "Did I ever say sex was *bad*?" I went on:

Sex is not bad. Sex is amazing—after you've stood before God and professed your vows of marriage in that commitment and trust. But any time before that, you are actually putting yourself (your emotional and sexual desires) above the other person. There is physical and emotional use going on, whether either of you recognize this or not. On the other hand, dying to yourself and putting the good of other first in this manner is one of the ultimate ways you can show the depth of your love for the other person.

She stared at me, trying to soak in what I was saying. Then I gently asked her, "Tell me, on those nights that you've slept with someone, after you've had sex and you go to leave, after you walk out that door, how do you feel?" She looked up at me with tears in her eyes and whispered, "Awful."

Sex is powerful, and chastity is not easy. Chastity is the virtue that frees us to love the other person for who he or she is, not just what he or she can do for us. If you've made the commitment (or recommitment) to save yourself for your spouse and to give all of yourself on your wedding night, you have to be ready for the battle. You know the battle because you have been with me through every step of this book, and you are aware and understand the profound ramifications of use, both emotionally and physically. You know that a life of virtue, faith, and pure intentions are the keys not only to true happiness, but to true love.

Chastity just makes sense. If you truly love someone in the way this book tries to lay out, then it wouldn't make sense to unite yourself to someone who hasn't run the race with you, to someone who hasn't proven over time that they will protect you. True love entails that we not say things with our bodies that we can't back up with our commitment —and that commitment is only sealed in marriage.

Your words can't say one thing and your body another. Many people confide in me that their significant other pressures them into sex or sexual activity by telling them, "If you really loved me, you'd show me," or even "I love you. I want to prove it to you." It can be so easy to get trapped into the emotions and passions connected to sexual desires, and it is a very slippery slope. A couple might start off with the best of intentions: holding hands and watching movies together, but three months later (or three days later), a couple may find themselves in that same room going much further than they had ever expected—wondering both "How did we get here?" and "Is either one of us going to stop?"

In sharing all this with a group of college men and women, I bluntly said, "You can't rev someone's engine only to turn it off," and to my surprise, the group started cheering. Yes, cheering. I have a feeling there were many in that room who had felt the negative effects of sliding down that slippery slope one too many times. Before the vow and commitment is made in marriage, any sexual act that is aimed at the arousal of the other hurts the relationship and the person—it's teasing, it's tempting, it's tormenting—it's not fair, and it's not love. And it definitely doesn't help you become the person you truly long to be.

In the eyes of the world, I know that what I am asking sounds radical, but this whole book is radical in the eyes of the world. If radical is loving selflessly, freely, and totally —not using someone for the way they make you feel, but loving them for who they truly are—then I want to be radical. If radical is saying, "I'll do anything for you, because I truly love you and want what's best for you, and I am going to prove this to you by safeguarding your purity with every fiber of my being," then I want to be radical. If a man or woman can love you in this way, make this commitment to you, they can do anything for you, and it is radical.

Striving for the virtue of chastity and learning to love someone through sacrificing your sexual desires before marriage will help make your marriage unshakable. And it will prepare you for those times of sacrifice in marriage. Seriously, if someone can do this for you before marriage, what couldn't they do for you?

A love that strives for chastity is a *selfless* love. And it allows the Formula for Moving Forward to operate most clearly and sincerely. We mentioned earlier that sexual activity is a binding and blinding force—and it is meant to bind a married couple together. But when people engage in sexual activity before marriage, it can often blind a couple, and keep people together who perhaps would be better off going their separate ways; indeed, sex can make a couple feel much closer than they really are. On the other hand, those who save themselves for marriage (or recommit to saving themselves for marriage) seldom regret it. It allows them to build their relationships on a sturdier foundation and enables them to discern more clearly the reality of their relationship through things such as the Formula for Moving Forward.

This book is largely about navigating relationships and dating, so as to live a life without regret. That is, to live a life with eyes wide open, with Emotional Virtue—beginning with the end in mind and focused on the most important things in life.

These are the steps of the Natural Progression of a Relationship: Acquaintances, True Friends, Defining the Relationship—Having a DTR, Dating, Courting, Engagement, and Marriage. Many who have taken them to heart and put them into practice have found them to be an avenue of great peace, joy, and clarity. At the very least, they contribute to a drama-free life—keeping us centered on what really matters, which is the key to happiness and the secret to building relationships that will last a lifetime.

CONCLUSION

In the Introduction, I mentioned that I hoped that by the end of this book you would hold in your hands some answers and a new outlook on life, and this is still my prayer. I pray that you no longer feel alone in your secret, silent battle. I pray that by calling out the World's Idea of Perfect, the Emoticoaster, and the Cycle of Use, you are able to see with eyes wide open the attacks that invade your heart and mind. By coming face-to-face with the Choice between love as only a feeling and love as a selfless act of the will, I hope you have been able to sort out not only what might have gone wrong in the past, but how to move forward with a whole new vision for love and relationships.

As we've said, there is no Altar Switch, and you no longer need to rely on the hope that there is one: virtue, especially Emotional Virtue, as well as being the "boss of your thoughts," are your new weapons to fight back against the attacks and assaults on your heart and mind. The Simply Irresistible lists and all the virtues are yours for the taking, to guide you in your pursuit of protecting and respecting the people in your life and to help form and shape you into the person you are striving to become.

I don't have to tell you that this life is not easy; even with this new plan for life and love in place, it will still be hard. That is why Finding Your Posse—your accountability partners—is so important, those friends will run and train with you in the Game of Life.

Women need the support and encouragement of other women to be there for them when they are tempted to run into the arms of a man in order to fill an insecurity, or to take away feelings of loneliness or pain. And men need other men as a band of brothers to go to battle with against temptations, to help them see the truth in the midst of lies, and to encourage them as they strive to protect and respect the women in their life.

The strong female posse and the strong male posse also need each other—to learn what authentic friendship looks like, to practice virtue, and to be that "check" for each other in terms of our Modesty of Intentions and our own growth in virtue. This community of friendship will provide the natural foundations for building a solid dating relationship.

When a relationship does start to form, we will be able to avoid the drama and the games, because we will take the risk of sincerity and clarity. This will take courage; but it will also help to minimize the Gray Area, bringing about much greater joy and much less heartache in the end.

Being aware of *what* sends you on the Emoticoaster and into the Cycle of Use, and what keeps you in the fog of the Gray Area, will help you sort out the confusion and frustration that sometimes comes from the effects of media, social media, texting, and all the rest. You know what messes with you; you know what tempts you and leads you down paths that you never intended to take. Strive to make the virtuous decision way before you ever find yourself in that compromising situation. Begin with the end in mind. You know who you want to be, what you are living for, and who you are living for. Now make your decisions, big and small, based on whether they take you closer or further away from the person you are striving to be.

Make use of the Formula for Moving Forward: God, virtue, time, trust, and honesty; it will be a sure guide as you navigate the Natural Progression of a Relationship, and even if you endure a breakup. As you move forward through the steps on the Natural Progression, I want you to wring out every ounce of joy, peace, fun, and excitement that each stage has to offer. Don't rush through them or wish them away. Each step is there for a reason—not only as a safeguard to move along at the right pace, but also for you to enjoy the full richness of each stage of the relationship. The memories made on the journey of any relationship are truly a priceless treasure.

I pray that you share this book with your friends, posse, family, school, significant other—anyone! Tell them about your new plan, your new awareness, and your new outlook on life and love.

And as you encounter those hard times and trials in life—the pain of a breakup, disappointments, mistakes, bouts with despair, anxiety, illness, losing loved ones, and a million other sorrows—remember, you are not alone. Not only do you have those around you, but you always have our Lord. More than anything else in this book, I pray that you will take with you the understanding that God loves you more than you could ever know. See your dignity and worth through His eyes. See yourself the way He sees you. Take all the worries of this life and Lay It All Down at His feet. He loves you just the way you are, but too much to leave you that way. He wants to love you, listen to you, heal your pain and help you grow, make you strong, and run with you. He will fill you with His life. He has a plan for your life and He has called you to greatness. Above all, *you can trust Him*—you can trust Him to heal your past; you can trust Him with your future; and you can trust Him with your life.

Keep fighting the good fight—it is so worth it! I am excited for you to embark on this new journey. You will never regret living this life of virtue, this life of love, this life of faith.

I promise, it will not disappoint you.

Know that I am praying for you and that you are loved,

Sarah Swafford

DISCUSSION QUESTIONS

Part I: The Attack:
Where Is All This Coming From?

Chapter 1: The World's Idea of Perfect

1. Where do you think the "World's Idea of Perfect" comes from? What attributes would you say make up the "World's Idea of Perfect" for women? And for men?

2. What does competition and comparing look like in your life? Have you ever felt like you are not "enough," or even "invisible"?

3. How do you think the media, and especially social media, play a role in the pressures of the "World's Idea of Perfect" and what it means to "make it" in life? When you hear good news about others, what is your first reaction? Are you happy for them, or do you consider their good somehow to be your loss?

4. Do you see any connection between the material in this chapter and the challenges to forming authentic friendships?

Chapter 2: The Emoticoaster

1. It is often said that men and women have a hard time understanding one another. What are some ways that men and women are different when it comes to relationships and communication?

2. What does the Typical Friday Night illustrate? For the women, can you relate to this night and its aftermath? For the men, how is this different from your Typical Friday Night?

3. The Emoticoaster (Mental Stalking, Social Media Stalking, Flirting, Texting, Calling, and Physically Stalking) may look different for men and women, but it can definitely be a reality for both sexes. How have you seen the Emoticoaster play out—maybe in your own life, or in the lives of others?

4. What are some of the potential traps of the Emoticoaster? How can the Emoticoaster drown out other important parts of life?

Chapter 3: The Cycle of Use

1. How does the media attract and affect men and women differently? How does the media influence our desires and wants?

2. What do you think sends people onto the Cycle of Use? How important is self-knowledge? It may be helpful to privately take note of your own personal triggers.

3. St. John Paul II once said that the opposite of love is not hate, but use. What do you think he means by this?

4. Why is it so difficult to talk about "use"—being used and using others? Do you think being able to name "use" when it occurs and being able to recognize it for what it is might help to break this cycle?

Chapter 4: The Choice

1. What does the interior battle look like for men? How about a woman's interior battle? How does "use"—for

example, in "Getting Game" or even the "intoxication" of texting—play into these battles?

2. Why do you think there is so much confusion about what love really is? What was your reaction when you read: "Love is not primarily a feeling, but may be accompanied by a feeling"?

3. Why is it important to put love to "the test" and ask yourself: "Are my actions helping to foster what is best for the other person, or is it really about me and more about how the other person makes me feel?"

4. What does it mean to be responsible for someone else? Is it possible that true love means loving the other person so much that you would deny them what they might want in the moment because it's actually not what is best for them?

Part II: The Answer:
Where Do We Go from Here?

Chapter 5: The Altar Switch

1. Why do you think there is so much pressure to date and be in a relationship? Why is dating seen as such a status symbol in our society? Why is it easy for single people to feel so consumed by the 80-20 Problem and Its Big Three?

2. What would happen if we spent more time focused on Real Life's Big Three? Take some time to write out your goals and roles.

3. How important is the Game of Life and Real Life's Big Three in avoiding the negative effects of the Emoticoaster? How does getting Real Life's Big Three in line affect our perspective on dating and relationships?

4. What do you think of your time being single (either in the present or in the past)? How hard is it not to wish it away? How does focusing on *striving to become the woman of your dreams,* or focusing on *what kind of man you are called to be* change the way you approach life without an Altar Switch?

Chapter 6: What Is Emotional Virtue?

1. How do virtue and the freedom to love go together? How might having a concern for what is best for the other person serve as a guide for Emotional Virtue?

2. If we always asked ourselves, "Who do I want to be?" before we made every decision (and sincerely followed through on it), how often would we regret our choices? On the other hand, if we separate our actions from the person we claim to be, will we be more likely to make regrettable decisions? Why?

3. Why do you think emotions sometimes get a bad rap? How is "ordering" our emotions different from merely "suppressing" them?

4. How does anchoring your emotional enjoyment in sincere love for the other person help your love to deepen? What does it mean to say that even the "experience" of love goes to the next level when it takes place in the context of a love committed to the good of the other person?

Chapter 7: Simply Irresistible

1. Why do you think so much effort is spent on the World's Idea of Perfect and the checklists of success, fame, money, power, good looks, and admiration? Most of the Simply Irresistible lists pertain to character and virtue—

which are more attainable than good looks, wealth, and power. So why not focus on what is: a) more important; b) more deeply attractive; and c) more within our reach?

2. Were you surprised by the characteristics given by the opposite sex on the Simply Irresistible lists? If so, why?

3. It can be very difficult to come face to face with our weaknesses. Which items on the Simply Irresistible lists are the hardest for you? Which come more easily to you? And why is knowing yourself (self-knowledge) and having a personal awareness of your strengths and weaknesses so important in striving for a life of virtue?

4. Why are the Simply Irresistible lists for everyone, not just for single people?

Chapter 8: Lay It All Down

1. What are some of the masks that people wear? When people fall into despair from worry, scheming, comparing, manipulating, and so on, how does that affect the way they see themselves and their lives? Do you ever feel like you have to prove yourself to others, to yourself, or even to God?

2. What kinds of things do you think someone may need to drop off in the box at our Lord's feet? It might be good to privately start a list that you could take into confession with a priest or share with a trusted friend and let the forgiveness and healing start today.

3. How can making someone your "everything" or your "god" actually ruin your relationship? Why is that a burden that could break someone?

4. It has been said that the Devil's lie is twofold: in the beginning, he's our buddy tempting us; but in the end, he's the *accuser*, burying us in shame and feelings of

unworthiness. How does this relate to our being able to accept God's mercy and healing? Does God want us to "perfect" ourselves first and then come to Him, or does He want us to come to Him in our brokenness? Does it make sense to go to the doctor only when we are well? Or do we need to go to Him precisely when we are sick?

Part III: The Avenue: A Roadmap with the End in Mind

Chapter 9: Finding Your Posse

1. Why do you think it is so hard to find a solid group of friends? Why is it hard for women to trust other women, and for men to trust other men?

2. What are you looking for in a friend? Is there a balance between a friend loving you for who you are and one who challenges you to be the very best you can be? Why is it important not only to share your goals and dreams, but also to be vulnerable and share your struggles and weaknesses with your friends?

3. Given the perspective of growing in faith and virtue, what does it mean to be a true friend—one who truly loves and wills the good of the other? How might this affect what we are looking for in a friend?

4. Can you think of any examples in which accountability brings out the best in people?

Chapter 10: Don't Shoot the Messenger: The Modesty of Intentions

1. Did either of the opening stories (containing that statement, "If you can't control yourself, that's your own

problem") surprise you? What about the degree and intensity of the struggles of the opposite sex, as they were described in this chapter—did that surprise you?

2. In what ways can men exploit and manipulate women? How can women exploit and manipulate men? How does charity change the conversation of whether or not we should have concern for the struggles of the opposite sex?

3. Is there a relationship between our desire for the World's Idea of Perfect and the Modesty of Intentions?

4. Many have said that taking the Virtue Challenge, Cell Phone Challenge, and Closet Challenge has brought about a great sense of freedom. Why do you think this is? What are some other creative challenges that you could take in your life to help you grow in virtue and love?

Chapter 11: The Gray Area: Talking, Texting, and Hanging Out

1. Why do you think there are so many different views on the definition of dating in the twenty-first century?

2. How do you think texting and social media have affected dating? Why would it be wise not to get to know a person solely through texting or social media?

3. Some Gray Area is inevitable at the start of a relationship; but what are some of the ways in which a prolonged Gray Area causes confusion and sometimes heartache?

4. How can honesty and courage help to minimize the Gray Area?

Chapter 12: The Natural Progression of a Relationship

1. If all dating relationships either end in marriage or a breakup, why do you think the Natural Progression of a Relationship (and beginning with the end in mind) are important for navigating through relationships in the twenty-first century?

2. Why is having a network of shared friends helpful in a relationship, especially at the start of a new dating relationship? How about the importance of family here?

3. Why is having a DTR so important in the Natural Progression of a Relationship? Why might there need to be a second DTR? How do these two DTRs help to prevent prolonging the Gray Area unnecessarily?

4. Why should True Friends and Dating not look *drastically* different? And why is there a distinction between Dating and Courting?

5. Why is applying the Formula for Moving Forward so important at all the different steps in the Natural Progression of a Relationship?

6. How could you use this whole book and especially the Formula for Moving Forward to help during a breakup?

7. Marriage is the most important decision many will ever make in life; how does sexual activity before marriage affect the discernment of a couple heading into marriage?

8. How is chastity a great "yes," and not just a "no" to sexual activity?

9. How does the Natural Progression of a Relationship build a strong and sturdy foundation upon which to build a loving, lifelong marriage?

ACKNOWLEDGEMENTS

It would be impossible to thank everyone who has supported me on this journey and in my life, but please know of my deep appreciation for your love and kindness.

To my incredible husband Andy—or as I affectionately call him, Swaff—no words can express how much you mean to me. Your support and encouragement over the years has been invaluable and having a best friend, man of God, and in-house doctorate of theology to bounce ideas off of has been an unbelievable gift. Thank you for running this race of life by my side; saying "Hey" and "I do" to you were two of the best decisions I ever made. I love you more than you could ever know.

To my kids, thank you for your unconditional love. This book is for you, and I pray that when you read it someday, you will understand in your heart what it is that your Mama desires for you and has tried to show you all these years. And I love you more than you could ever know.

To my amazing and supportive parents, family, and extended family: my whole life you have always been the encouraging word, listening ear, and cheering section—you all mean so much to me. A special thanks to Mom and Dad for always having confidence in me and letting me come and sit at your quiet kitchen table on the farm and write.

To my extraordinary friends and the Atchison and Benedictine College communities, your support and generosity has been such an anchor in my life. Thank you for my formation. I know what a gift you are, and I will never take you for granted. A special thanks to Rita, Paige, Abby, and Erin—thank you for loving my family.

To everyone who shared their talents with me: to Jason, Crystalina, Jane, John, Devin, Chris, Jackie, all the kind souls who read through rough drafts, and to all of those prayer warriors who continue to go to battle with me— your kindness and the gift of your time is what helped make this book a reality.

And most of all, I would like to thank my Heavenly Father for sustaining me through this journey. You have taught me so much about myself, trust, courage, patience, endurance, surrender, and true love in writing this book. Thank you for the opportunity to share Your love, the intense love I have for You, and the joy of a life with You. I am truly blessed beyond words.

Emotional Virtue
SARAH SWAFFORD

It's time to THRIVE in your relationships, not just survive!

Reclaiming VIRTUE for a drama-free life!

Check out the website EMOTIONALVIRTUE.COM for more!

Connect with Sarah at emotionalvirtue.com
as well as on Twitter, Instagram, and Facebook: @sarahswafford18!

BRING THESE POWERFUL DISPLAYS TO YOUR CHURCH, SCHOOL, BUSINESS OR RETREAT CENTER, AND GIVE OTHERS THE CHANCE TO OBTAIN CHASTITY RESOURCES AND OTHER INSPIRATIONAL PRODUCTS BY VISITING

CHASTITYPROJECT.COM

GOT QUESTIONS? GET ANSWERS.

WATCH VIDEOS
GET RELATIONSHIP ADVICE
LAUNCH A PROJECT
READ ANSWERS TO TOUGH QUESTIONS
FIND HELP TO HEAL FROM THE PAST
LISTEN TO POWERFUL TESTIMONIES
SHOP FOR GREAT RESOURCES
SCHEDULE A SPEAKER

emotionalvirtue.com

FOR $2 OR LESS, WHO WOULD YOU GIVE THESE BOOKS AND CDS TO?

In order to reach as many people as possible, more than 20 chastity CDs and books (including the one you're reading) are available in bulk orders for $2 or less! Therefore, share this book and others like it with the people in your life who need it right now. For example:

YOUR COLLEGE DORM
YOUR HIGH SCHOOL
YOUR YOUTH OR YOUNG ADULT GROUP AT CHURCH
YOUR ALMA MATER

Buy a case of books and donate them as gifts at graduation, freshman orientation, retreats, conferences, confirmation, as a missionary effort through campus ministry, or to people you meet anywhere. You never know whose life you could change.

TO ORDER, VISIT

CHASTITY PROJECT.COM

If you want to help others to live a drama-free life, share this book with them for as little as

$3 per copy!

Think of those in your community who could benefit from reading it:

- Start a book study in your college dorm
- Give it away in your youth or young adult group
- Share copies with your Confirmation or religious ed classmates
- Study it in your high school religion class
- Distribute copies on retreats
- Offer it as a gift for graduations and birthdays
- Donate copies to your campus ministry program

For more information, please visit
www.chastityproject.com